PRAISE FOR I WISH I'D KNOWN

Tommy Briggs and I have been close friends for more than 30 years. He worked at my side for a number of years and gave oversight to prayer and counseling. Few people have the discernment and spiritual sensitivity that God has graced Tommy with. He understands the power in the spiritual realm of both darkness and light. He knows the importance of freedom and fullness in the power of God's Spirit. For these reasons and more, I'm convinced that the insights Tommy shares through this book will not only be an inspiration, but in many ways will lead you to a far more meaningful life — living in God's presence in the present.

~ **JAMES ROBISON**
President and Founder, LIFE Outreach International; author of *Indivisible* and *True Prosperity*

I have known Tommy Briggs since the 1970s and have admired him as a friend, co-worker and pastor. Tommy's integrity is beyond question. His story is filled with insights that can save the reader from unnecessary mistakes. When he speaks or writes, it is his heart that you encounter. I heartily recommend Tommy's story to all. Those who read it will be enriched handsomely. He deserves to be heard and read.

~ **DUDLEY HALL**
President of Successful Christian Living Ministries and Kerygma Ventures; author of *Grace Works* and *Incense and Thunder*

Tommy Briggs has brought insight and healing to thousands of people during his years as a pastor. I am so thankful he is looking back over a storied journey and reminding us of the sound wisdom and counsel God has imparted to him.

⁂ **BRADY BOYD**
Senior Pastor of New Life Church; author of *Fear No Evil* and *Sons and Daughters*

I have met few people in my life who can walk into a room and in five minutes have everyone listening to them for good reason. Tommy Briggs is one of those people. This book is like sitting down at a table for lunch with a hero who pours nearly eight decades of wisdom into you with the sensitivity of a loving father who's been where you are. It will serve as a reservation for two that will change the way you walk out your tomorrow and see your today. Enjoy your meal!

⁂ **PRESTON MORRISON**
Senior Pastor of Gateway Church Scottsdale

Tommy Briggs is a gift in my life and a gift to the church. No degree or title can replace years of faithful, generous service. He has earned the right to speak to us all by being surrendered and humble for decades of service to the Bride of Christ and the men and women who lead the church. More than having the right to speak to us, his years have given him great wealth to share with us all. The Apostle Paul says we have many teachers but few fathers. Here is a beautiful book by one of our few fathers. Open, read and receive.

⁂ **BOB HAMP**
Pastor of Freedom Ministry, Gateway Church; author of *Think Differently, Live Differently*

I sat down to read the first chapter and didn't move until I had read it all the way through! I felt as if Tommy was sitting across from me spinning out his amazing, grace-filled story and what he's learned as God moved. Laced with humor, down-to-earth wisdom and spiritual depth, this book captures truth in a delightful way.

᙭ **BARBARA BYERS, PH.D., LPC**

If ever a generation needed words of wisdom from an elder at the gate, it is now. Tommy Briggs brings a wonderful presentation of timely truths into the context of a society in moral free fall. His open candor and rock solid common sense make for stimulating reading. The fact that these spiritual discoveries come out of his own experiences makes the book most profitable. This work is like a treasured family heirloom.

᙭ **DOUG WHITE**
Former Senior Pastor of Restoration Church

In *I Wish I'd Known*, Tommy Briggs, a wise thoughtful father of the faith, shares with humor and candor profound stories that taught him life lessons. He skillfully reminds us that every day is a gift in which to get to know our Creator. Every reader will identify with some examples and cherish the wisdom to be gained by his example rather than our experience. Tommy and his late wife, Nancy, have been a tremendous encouragement as friends, counselors and prayer warriors to Robert and me.

᙭ **DEBBIE MORRIS**
Pastor of Pink (Gateway Women); author of
The Blessed Woman

I first heard Tommy Briggs share this message with a group of pastors gathered for a leadership event. As he shared these life lessons, much more was going on than simple instruction. Men and women were being fathered. Life and wisdom were being imparted with power and with much love. It was a holy moment. I knew right then that this message needed to be a book. My prayer is that this book will leave a legacy of holy moments, for we all need fathers, and they are few.

ᵃ ALAN SMITH
Associate Pastor of Freedom Ministry, Gateway Church; author of *Unveiled*

Tommy wrote this book as a living legacy for his family, but his open and honest stories of faith are a gift to all of us. His loving, grandfatherly voice will touch you deeply as he shares from his own journey of living faithfully as a child of God.

ᵃ SARAH GROEN-COLYN, PhD
Sanctuary Psychological Services

I WISH I'D KNOWN

Stories of Life & Faith

TOMMY BRIGGS

In memory of

MY WIFE, NANCY M. BRIGGS

&

MY GRANDSON, ADAM McCAULEY BAUGH

I WISH I'D KNOWN
STORIES OF LIFE AND FAITH

Published by Tommy H. Briggs, Sr.

Copyright © 2012 by Tommy H. Briggs, Sr.

ISBN 978-0-615-72099-9

Cover and Layout Design: Paul Sirmon for Buzzbomb Creative

Cover Photography: Alex Headrick

Printed in the United States of America.

I WISH I'D KNOWN
Stories of Life and Faith

ACKNOWLEDGEMENTS

I want to express appreciation to Joquin Baptist Church of Goshen, Alabama, the church I attended as a young boy. It was here I first attended church services and still remember my Sunday school teachers teaching me about the Lord. This church has a long history; thank you for remaining faithful to the Gospel even to this day.

I want to acknowledge with thanksgiving the impact of the churches who saw within me the pastoral gift and allowed me to be their Senior Pastor: New Hope Baptist Church in Double Springs, Alabama; Pisgah Baptist Church in Pisgah, Alabama; First Baptist Church in Cordova, Alabama; Head of Island Church in Head of Island, Louisiana; New Prospect Baptist Church in Jasper, Alabama; Haltom Road Baptist Church in Fort Worth, Texas; and Cross Timbers Church in Valley View, Texas.

I also have a deep love and appreciation for Dr. C. Douglas White and the staff and leadership of Restoration Church in Euless, Texas, who allowed me to serve for more than seventeen years as Associate Pastor. My tenure with you has changed my life forever.

I am now serving on the staff of Gateway Church in Southlake, Texas. Thank you Pastor Robert Morris, the Elders and the staff who administrate and live out Christianity in ways seldom seen in our present-day culture. I am so grateful to serve in the Department of Freedom Ministries at Gateway with Bob Hamp, Alan Smith, Rebecca Wilson, Linda Godsey, Aja Schiewe, Mike Brisky, Brady Daniel, Tracey Bennett, Cathy Ethridge, Alex Headrick, Katy Davis, Amy Jo Thompson and my personal assistant Julie Keaveny. You are my dream of what church life should be.

Then there are other ministries and leaders who have had a profound influence on my life, and I must say thank you to several of those also: James Robison of LIFE Outreach International; Dudley Hall of Successful Christian Living Ministries and Kerygma Ventures; Leanne Payne of Pastoral Care Ministry in Wheaton, Illinois; and Ministries of Pastoral Care of Peoria, Illinois. Thank you to Ardsley Park Baptist Church of Savannah, Georgia, who open their doors to the servicemen of Hunter Air Force Base. You are the church that helped me find the Lord and then licensed me to serve in His ministry. To Philadelphia Baptist Church in Birmingham, Alabama, for ordaining me in the ministry, thank you.

I also want to acknowledge the generosity of "Mama Hadwin" and her son, Lynn Hadwin, of Savannah, Georgia, who took me into their home after my discharge from the Air Force so I could save money for college. Thank you for believing in me.

I have a deep appreciation and love for those who endorsed this book for me. Thank you so much. It meant the world to me.

I am deeply grateful to Stacy Burnett for her skill and craft as she helped me put this book together. Thank you for your guidance, talent and encouragement.

Thank you to copyeditor S. George Thomas and proofreaders Joyce Freeman and Gwen Bolton for your skillful abilities. For photographer Alex Headrick for taking the cover photo of the trees in my backyard at sunset. For Paul Sirmon for beautifully designing and laying out the book, and for InProv for printing the book.

I am at a loss to find words to express thanks to my family of origin: my Dad, whose singing of Sacred Harp Music still lingers in my heart and mind. My Mom, whose prayers for me and faith in me brought me to find Jesus as my Savior. My brother, Woody, who served in World War II and thereby preserved freedom for me. My brother, Max, who was also a pastor and my closest friend during the last 30 years. They have all completed their earthly journeys and are with the Lord. My only living sibling, my sister, Sybileen, who continues to be with me in ministry through love and intercessory prayer for me.

My children and their spouses: Joe and Kellie Baugh; Tommy Jr. and Janna Briggs; Rich and Kerrie Wenzel. You are living proof of the faithfulness of the Lord. Your commitment to the kingdom of our Lord is the greatest gift any Father could ever receive.

My ten living grandchildren who are already demonstrating their love for the Lord and in many ways encourage me to finish well: Braden, Susannah, Gabriel, Graham, Taylor, Hayden, Carter, Emily, Jacob and Matthew. You are my heritage and gifts from the Lord. For my grandson, Adam, who only lived three years, but was a profound witness for the Lord during his short life.

And most of all, my wife, Nancy, who is now with the Lord, taught me so much about loyalty, purity, unconditional love and commitment in the 46 years of marriage we shared together. I will always love you.

FOREWORD

✢ *ROBERT MORRIS* ✢

I have known Tommy Briggs for 30 years. He is one of my closest friends and a true spiritual father. In the most difficult times of my life, I call Tommy and he always provides wise, gracious counsel. I can tell you from years of experience that his character is absolutely above reproach and his ability to spiritually guide others is phenomenal.

Since he joined the Gateway Church staff in 2007, I've often joked that I brought him on simply so I could keep my personal counselor nearby whenever I need him! Unsurprisingly, he proved to be one of the best possible additions to our staff. I'm so grateful to work side by side with him. It's one of the greatest privileges of my life.

Debbie and I have so many fond memories of Tommy and his wife, Nancy, who passed away in 2010. We were both mentored and discipled by this amazing couple. When Debbie spoke at events for Pink (Gateway's Women's Ministry), Nancy would always attentively listen and smile, leaving no doubt in Debbie's mind that Nancy was for her.

Nancy was sent from heaven to be a great and incredible wife to Tommy and a wonderful mother to their children. When she went to be with the Lord, she did so with great grace. I often share at memorial services that believers don't say "goodbye," but "I will see you later," because we will all be reunited in heaven. The last time I visited Nancy at the hospital, I said "goodbye" out of habit, but she replied, "No, Pastor Robert, I will see you later."

Her funeral was a beautiful celebration of a life well lived. We truly got a glimpse of what heaven will be like. Most of all, I will never forget what Tommy shared. He said that in Nancy's final days, he asked the Lord, "If you are going to take her, can I go too?" The Lord responded, "No, I'm not finished with you yet." Tommy took that to mean the Lord wanted to heal him of some heart issues before he followed Nancy. I'm going to be bold and suggest it also meant the Lord still has more for Tommy to do on this earth.

That brings me to this book. I firmly believe this book is one of the reasons the Lord said, "I'm not finished with you yet." Tommy told me once that his job as a counselor and pastor is to simply remove obstacles that are in the way of people having an intimate relationship with their Lord Jesus Christ. He has removed obstacles for so many and this book is an opportunity for him to remove those obstacles for you. I urge you to listen to the wisdom he has to offer. Learn from his lessons. Most of all, be encouraged by His close relationship with the Lord and let it transform your relationship with Him.

Although Tommy misses Nancy dearly, he continues to serve the King with all his might, soul and strength. Only heaven knows for sure how many people's lives have been changed by Tommy's influence. One day, when the Lord is finished with him, Tommy will join Nancy with the Lord. I believe he will walk the streets of gold and countless people will come up to him and say, "Pastor Tommy, thank you. You helped me so much! You brought me closer to the Lord!" Because you're reading this book, I know you will be one of those people. The truth in this man has changed my life forever. Allow it to change yours, too.

ROBERT MORRIS
Founding Senior Pastor of Gateway Church
Dallas/Fort Worth, Texas;
Author of *The Blessed Life, From Dream to Destiny, The Power of Your Words* and *The God I Never Knew*

I WISH I'D KNOWN WHEN I CONFESS MY SINS THEY ARE REALLY FORGIVEN

As far as the east is from the west, so far has He removed our transgressions from us.

▶ Psalm 103:12

"Harvey! Get up! Come out here!" A man's voice called out as he pounded his fist on our front door.

I sat straight up in bed as the sound of the pounding resounded throughout our very small three-room home. It was the middle of the night, and I had been sound asleep. Immediately, I jumped out of bed and followed my dad out to the front porch to find out who was causing the ruckus. It was our neighbor, and he was upset about something. Before my dad could even ask what was wrong, the man said, "Listen!"

The three of us stood quietly on the front porch; we could hear music playing from a piano in the small Baptist church across the road from our house. We lived in Joquin, a rural community in Southern Alabama between Troy and Goshen, where everybody knew everybody and things didn't change much. And we knew this was *not* normal. All the lights were off in the church … it was as though the piano was playing by itself in the dark.

There was a graveyard behind the church, and I'd heard countless stories about the ghosts and spirits that lived there. My father had once told me a story about the time he and a friend had to walk by the church graveyard as they were coming home late one night after working in the field. As my dad looked over toward the cemetery, he saw something glowing in the dark. Then it just disappeared. Then he saw it again. And then it was gone. Frightened and confused, my dad couldn't figure out what it was, but *something* was intermittently glowing in the dark. He convinced his friend to go

"WE LIVED IN JOQUIN … WHERE EVERYBODY KNEW EVERYBODY AND THINGS DIDN'T CHANGE MUCH."

down to the graveyard with him to see what was going on. The glow turned out to be a drifter sitting on top of one of the graves smoking a cigar. Every time he took a puff, the cigar would glow in the dark. When my dad's friend asked him what he was doing in the cemetery at night, he said, "Cemeteries are the safest place in the world to sleep. Nobody's ever going to bother you!"

People in Joquin never visited cemeteries at night because there was a theory that spirits and ghosts of the dead roamed around the graveyard. Down the road from our Baptist church was Camp Ground Methodist Church. The Camp Ground Methodist Graveyard was across the road from the church, and most people in town believed a spirit named Camp Ground "booger" lived there. People who drove by there at night told stories about seeing Camp Ground "booger" rise up out of the ground and walk toward them. They were so terrified; they'd get out of there as fast as they could!

As I stood on the front porch, I began to imagine ghosts and spirits flying around the church. I grew *very* afraid. I wondered if the Camp Ground "booger" had moved over to *our* graveyard. *Maybe he was the one playing the piano,* I thought. I decided to stay on the front porch while my dad and our neighbor went over to the church to find out who (or what) was playing the piano. Just like the time before, it turned out to be a drifter who had been walking along the countryside going from one place to another. He told them he just wanted to rest a while, and when he saw the piano, he decided to play a few songs to rest his soul.

> *"PEOPLE WHO DROVE BY THERE AT NIGHT TOLD STORIES ABOUT SEEING CAMP GROUND 'BOOGER' RISE UP OUT OF THE GROUND AND WALK TOWARD THEM."*

I was filled with such fear that night. It caused me to become afraid of the church *and* of God and made me very fearful of the spiritual world. In my young mind, graveyards and churches were related, so if graveyards were creepy, churches were creepy. During this time of my life, fear developed in the way I related to God, because God existed in this mysterious, spiritual realm and yet He was very real.

I grew up going to that Baptist church down the road from our house. Whenever the pastor gave an invitation at the close of his message, I always felt like I needed to go forward to confess my sins or, at the very least, pray at the altar. Every summer, our church had a revival, and it almost seemed as though people couldn't get saved any other time. In fact, it was expected that everyone would get saved during the revival. If I didn't go forward during the revival meetings, it was only because I had gone down during the last meeting and I was holding on as tightly as I could to the back of the wooden pew to keep myself from walking to the front one more time.

This scenario repeated itself throughout my life. I'd make a profession of faith several times a year and *always* at the revival. I was even baptized twice before I turned 18. Fear of the church and God, along with false guilt, kept me going back to the altar again and again. But because I was motivated by fear, I never really made a true, heartfelt commitment to the Lord. I now know it was because I never understood the cleansing power of confessing sin.

> "FEAR OF THE CHURCH AND GOD, ALONG WITH FALSE GUILT, KEPT ME GOING BACK TO THE ALTAR AGAIN AND AGAIN."

My relationship with God was like a broken record.

"I'm sorry, God."

"You're forgiven."

"I'm sorry, God."

"You're forgiven."

Every time I took a trip down to the altar, I was really telling the Lord I was sorry for whatever sin I'd committed that day. I didn't understand the minute I confessed my sins, He had forgiven me for all of them. I was already forgiven! I was free from guilt.

I had a misunderstanding of what true forgiveness was and how forgiveness comes about. I realize now it was my lack of understanding how sins are forgiven and pardoned. When you really confess your sins, God forgives them.

The Lord paid the price for our sins when He sacrificed His life on the cross. Before He died, He said, "It is finished." Because of His work on the cross, the Lord has provided you with a place where you can put your sin and *know* you no longer have to carry the burden of it anymore. 1 John 1:8–9 says, "If we say that we have no sin, we deceive ourselves, and the truth is not in us. If we confess our sins, He is faithful and just to forgive us our sins and to cleanse us from all unrighteousness."

When you give your life over to God through a relationship with Jesus Christ, your life is literally in the hands of Almighty God, the Ruler of this Universe. No one can get Him to turn you loose. I once heard a Southern Baptist missionary by the name of Miss Bertha Smith say, "It's not a matter of you having ahold of God, it's that God has ahold of you." It's not about *my* ability to hold on to God; it's about who God is and what the Bible says about Him. Almighty God, Creator of this Universe, has ahold of *me*! I'm His son, and He will not let go! In fact, He says in His Word, "neither shall any man pluck them out of my hand" (John 10:28, KJV).

I wished I'd understood that when I came to a personal relationship with Almighty God through Jesus Christ, He took ahold of my life and won't ever let go! Even in my darkest moments, when I've been disobedient and feel like I've failed God and feel distant from God, those are the very moments when God shows up. Those are the moments when I don't expect Him to be anywhere near me, but I hear Him and sense His presence wooing me back. He won't let me go! And He won't let you go!

> "I WISHED I'D UNDERSTOOD THAT WHEN I CAME TO A PERSONAL RELATIONSHIP WITH ALMIGHTY GOD THROUGH JESUS CHRIST, HE TOOK AHOLD OF MY LIFE AND WON'T EVER LET GO!"

Years ago, I memorized a little saying: "A faith that fizzles before it's finished was faulty from the first." There's an eternal truth in that little phrase. Because I used to believe out of fear and guilt, my faith was faulty. I now know when I confess my sins, I'm really forgiven. My relationship with the Lord is no longer based in fear, but in faith (Romans 10:17). Faith in God is truly through His Son the Lord Jesus Christ, and it is Almighty God who has ahold of *me*, not the other way around.

If you're one of God's children and Jesus is the Lord of your life, but you're sinning, I'm fully convinced the Holy Spirit woos you back to the Father. As Christians, we cannot get away with sin and be right with God. If I want to rebel against God, I suffer the consequences of my wrong decisions and my disobedience. But if I want to stay in fellowship with God, I've got to get right; I've got to be repentant. At this phase in my life, I've learned to do that quickly because I don't want to miss the presence of God.

Not too long ago, I was in my living room talking to the Lord about all the things going on in my life. I felt like there were many areas of my life that weren't aligned with Him, such as my thought patterns. As I was praying, the Lord asked me, "Would you like to know what it feels like for Me to lift my hand away from you?"

Instantly, before I could even answer Him, I felt it. I felt the emptiness, the darkness and the absolute abandonment, for just a split second. I fell to my knees with my face on the ground and cried out, "God, no! I don't want to know." Instantly, I repented and asked Him to realign my life with His.

> "AS CHRISTIANS, WE CANNOT GET AWAY WITH SIN AND BE RIGHT WITH GOD."

I do my best to walk in repentance. When I know I'm wrong and I've sinned, I get back on my knees and say, "God, I'm wrong. I know I want Your presence. I can feel Your presence withdrawing because I've been walking away from You. But I want to be right with You as quickly as I possibly can."

I'm confident that as a believer and child of God, I can't get away with things. God won't let me alone. Praise God, He won't let me alone! He never lets go.

CHAPTER 2

I WISH I'D KNOWN MY INWARD HEART WAS MORE IMPORTANT THAN MY OUTWARD APPEARANCE

But the Lord said to Samuel, "Do not look at his appearance or at his physical stature, because I have refused him. For the Lord does not see as man sees; for man looks at the outward appearance, but the Lord looks at the heart."

➤ 1 Samuel 16:7

When I was a little boy, I had freckles on my face. And not just a few freckles … massive amounts of freckles! It was so bad the guys at school would yell out, "Hey, freckled-faced kid!" And that was just *one* of my features I was teased about. I was also called a slim Jim, a skinny freckled-face, a bean pole and the list goes on.

I rode the bus to and from school every day, and once on the bus ride home, the other kids began teasing me and making fun of my appearance. I was so humiliated and hurt by their teasing that as soon as the bus pulled over to my stop and I got off, I started crying. When I got home, my mother tried consoling me by saying, "When they tease you about your freckles, you tell them your mother wouldn't take a million dollars for every single one of them on your face!" While her words built up my confidence and encouraged me, I still hated my freckles! And I still felt different from everyone else.

I always worried a great deal about not looking like other boys my age; and not just because of my physical features, but also the way I dressed. We lived on a farm, and my family was dirt poor. We couldn't afford to buy new shoes or clothes very often, but my mother taught us the importance of cleanliness and keeping the things we did own nice and neat. I may have had holes in the soles of my shoes or patches on my overalls, but they were clean. In our household, there was always an emphasis on cleanliness and dressing to the best of your ability.

> "I ALWAYS WORRIED A GREAT DEAL ABOUT NOT LOOKING LIKE OTHER BOYS MY AGE; AND NOT JUST BECAUSE OF MY PHYSICAL FEATURES, BUT ALSO THE WAY I DRESSED."

By the time I got to high school, I was well over six feet tall. People would walk up to me, look up in the air and ask, "How's the weather up there?" I cannot put in print some of the replies I learned to give those people. (Let's just say it was before my salvation experience, and it wasn't nice at all!) It was my way of retaliating at them for kidding me about my size. It may have been funny to them, but I was sensitive about my appearance.

If people weren't asking about the weather, they were asking me if I was going to play basketball. Everyone expected me to play sports since I was tall, but I was thin and not very athletic. Then, the summer before my senior year of high school, my father passed away. My mother and I moved into town away from the farm, and I got a job working at Foster Brothers' Manufacturing Company where they made pants for men and boys. I had to work as many hours as possible in order to help with living expenses, which meant I had to work during my PE period. Not only that, but the coaches didn't give me the time of day. They only reached out to guys who were physically disciplined and had developed a muscular, athletic body. I began to look at those other guys with an envious attitude. In my heart, I'd ask, "God, why did You give me a body like this?!"

I went through high school trying to overcome the stigma everybody had put on me — I was tall, I wasn't athletic, we were poor, I had to work during my PE period. I never felt like my peers. I always felt different.

"I NEVER FELT LIKE MY PEERS. I ALWAYS FELT DIFFERENT."

As soon as I got my first paycheck from Foster Brothers', I went out and bought the most stylish clothes I could find. I wanted to be neat, clean and dressed appropriately. I spent a lot of money on clothes and shoes, my favorite being a pair of white bucks. I was always so worried about how I looked. I had made up my mind that if I looked good and had fashionable clothes and good-looking shirts that I'd be more accepted by others. This feeling I had about wearing stylish clothes and looking my best carried over to my young adult years.

When I entered the Air Force (you'll read more about that later), I learned how to shine my shoes and dress neatly. I always made sure my pants and shirts were starched and ironed as required. The Air Force regulations said we had to be inspected every day. They checked to make sure our fingernails were clean, that we'd washed behind our ears, that our uniforms were pressed and anything else they could think of. There became an increased emphasis on how I looked outwardly, and the more I fell in line with the military disciplines, the better I felt about myself. The focus was completely on my outward appearance.

One of the disciplines we worked on when I was in the Air Force was learning how to perfectly march in formation as a squadron. That meant we had a certain number of men in rows across and back. We even had a person who set the cadence for the squadron. I didn't like it at all, because I was always placed in the front row of the right-hand column, behind the person who set the cadence who was *always* the shortest guy in the squadron. Being 6'5", I had to discipline myself not to step on him, because my legs were almost as long as he was tall! Even there, I felt singled out because of my size.

Then one day, I discovered a story in the Bible that gave me hope. In 1 Samuel 16:7, "the Lord said to Samuel, 'Do not look at his appearance or at his physical stature, because I have refused him. *For the Lord does not see as man sees; for man looks at the outward appearance, but the Lord looks at the heart'*" (emphasis added). I realized I had been working on my outward appearance all those years, but God was looking at my heart.

Growing up, my mother did her best to encourage me not to worry about what others said, but no one ever told me God Himself had fashioned how my body developed and looks weren't as important as my inner character. No one ever told me God looked at my heart rather than my outward appearance. I wish I'd known my "different" look was given to me by God to make me stand out in any crowd. That it was all part of His plan.

If I'd known as a young man that my outward appearance wasn't as important as my inward heart, I'd have spent more time working on my heart. I'd have spent more time becoming more like Jesus and not worried about how many freckles I had or whether my pants were perfectly pressed.

In 1 Samuel 8, we read the story of the process the prophet Samuel went through when he was selecting Saul as king. Until this time, Israel had been judged by judges and not kings, and the sons of Samuel were appointed as leaders and judges over Israel.

> "NO ONE EVER TOLD ME GOD LOOKED AT MY HEART RATHER THAN MY OUTWARD APPEARANCE."

13

The Bible is clear that Samuel's sons didn't walk in the ways of the Lord, so the people became displeased with them and came to Samuel "and said to him, 'Look, you are old, and your sons do not walk in your ways. Now make us a king to judge us like all the nations'" (1 Samuel 8:5).

Instead of seeking the Lord for His wisdom and discernment about what needed to be done with the sons of Samuel, the people of Israel wanted to be like other nations around them. They were looking at the outward appearance of things. They were looking at how other nations stood out because of the way their kings appeared.

"But the thing displeased Samuel when they said, 'Give us a king to judge us.' So Samuel prayed to the Lord. And the Lord said to Samuel, 'Heed the voice of the people in all that they say to you; for they have not rejected you, but they have rejected Me, that I should not reign over them'" (1 Samuel 8:6–7).

Whenever you look at the outward appearance of things rather than looking at the internal position of someone's heart or your own heart, that's when you're prone to turn your heart away from God and make a decision against the will of the Lord.

And because the people of Israel chose to make their own demands instead of seeking His will, the Lord said, "Go ahead and appoint them a king according to their desires. But you will tell them what will happen when they have this king." And so Samuel outlined for them what was going to happen. He told them a king would use the people, their produce, their sons and their daughters for his own personal gain and for his own personal glory rather than for the glory of the Lord. Even after Samuel warned them, the people refused to obey the voice of Samuel and said, "No, we will have a king to rule over us." Obviously, they wanted to be like the other nations of the world rather than to stand out as God intended.

In the end, Samuel appointed Saul and anointed him to be king. The summary of what happened in Saul's reign is recorded for us in 1 Samuel 15:23 when Samuel discovered Saul had actually lied about what he had done with the spoils of his battles. Saul kept back the best of the sheep and the oxen under the pretense of sacrificing them to the Lord and giving Him the best of the spoils as a sacrifice, but in reality, Saul intended to keep them for himself. And so Samuel came and told Saul, "For rebellion is as the sin of witchcraft, and stubbornness is as iniquity and idolatry. Because you have rejected the word of the Lord, He has also rejected you from being king."

When we look at someone's outward appearance and the way their bodies look rather than looking at the internal structure of their heart, we are prone to make decisions and choices that will ultimately cause us to rebel against the Lord. The foundation of our choices and decisions need to be in keeping with the Lord's will for our lives.

> "THE FOUNDATION OF OUR CHOICES AND DECISIONS NEED TO BE IN KEEPING WITH THE LORD'S WILL FOR OUR LIVES."

As it applies to my own life, I made choices based on my outward appearance and the way other people looked at me, because I was looking at my outward appearance and my experiences growing up. And because I didn't walk in the will of the Lord and made choices that were against His will for my life, it ultimately proved to be a source of great pain, heartbreak and agony that took me years to overcome.

The good news is there's still more to the story of Samuel and the people of Israel. When Samuel went among the sons of Jesse to select a replacement for Saul, "the Lord said to Samuel, 'Do not look at his appearance or at his physical stature, because I have refused him. For the Lord does not see as man sees; for man looks at the outward appearance, but the Lord looks at the heart'" (1 Samuel 16:7). The Lord told that to Samuel after he looked at all of the sons of Jesse to find a king, and he found none. They were all good-looking and of the right stature. From outward appearances, any of them could be king. But ultimately, Samuel selected David, a short, ruddy looking guy. The Lord was looking at his inward heart, not his outward appearance, and in him, He saw a man after His own heart: "He raised up for them David as king, to whom also He gave testimony and said, 'I have found David the son of Jesse, a man after My own heart, who will do all My will'" (Acts 13:22–23).

"OF ALL THE PEOPLE IN THE PICTURE, THERE WERE ONLY TWO PEOPLE SMILING: ME AND ONE OTHER LADY."

Remember the athletes I envied in high school? I saw them again at my fortieth class reunion. Not everyone was able to come (and some were no longer living), but those who were there took a class picture together. When I received my picture in the mail a few weeks later, something stood out to me as I looked at it. Of all the people in the picture, there were only two people smiling: me and one other lady. These guys I had been envious of and had admired so much because they were athletic and seemingly economically better off than my family, now looked tired and weary with no glow at all in their countenance. You see, it's about who I am on the inside; my character. It's all about the heart.

CHAPTER 3

I WISH I'D KNOWN MY SEXUALITY IS NOT MY TRUE IDENTITY

"Once you had no identity as a people; now you are God's people. Once you received no mercy; now you have received God's mercy."

✦ *1 Peter 2:10* (NLT)

My father was a good man and was well-respected in our community. He was a sharecropper well-known for being a hard worker who took care of his family. As a sharecropper, my father didn't own any property; instead, he farmed another man's land. (In fact, he never owned a piece of property in his life.) I was the youngest of four kids — two brothers and one sister — and as a part of a sharecropper's family, it was customary for the boys to quit school and work on the farm. My two older brothers did just that. They quit school when they were teenagers and went to work with my dad on the farm. When they became adults, they left home, went into the military and, later, got other jobs.

As early as five years old, I knew I didn't want to quit school to help my dad with the farm. So, when I was in elementary school, I set a goal for my life: to finish high school. I wanted to *be somebody*, and being somebody meant I finished high school.

There was an expectation that I would quit school and go to work on the farm. I believed my father loved me and he was just desperately trying to make a living for our family, but I also knew in my heart I wasn't doing what he wanted me to do. My mother, on the other hand, encouraged me to stay in school. She even worked on the farm in my place in order for me to complete high school. But since that was contradictory to what my father wanted, an emotional separation arose between my father and me when I was still very young.

> "I WANTED TO BE SOMEBODY, AND BEING SOMEBODY MEANT I FINISHED HIGH SCHOOL."

My father also had a raging temper and, at times, would get really angry and lash out. I have many painful memories of his outbursts. He usually took his anger out on the farm animals, but there were times he would verbally abuse my mother and us kids. (I say this not to be judgmental or critical, but rather as a means of revealing what I now believe to be generational weakness or family line curses that were passed on to my generation.) Because of his anger and rage, I grew up fearing him. This fear was yet another driving force that separated me emotionally from my father.

Because my father didn't model emotional control to me, I also had anger issues I had to deal with in my early adulthood. By God's grace, I've found victory in these areas through understanding the character and nature of my heavenly Father who is so unlike my earthly father in most of His ways.

Sadly, my father passed away the summer after my junior year of high school, long before we could ever have a true father/son relationship. There were important formative and foundational issues absent in my relationship with him. He was not a part of my late teenage years and, in many ways, my father was absent even before he died. Because my brothers had already left home, I had no male guidance in my life at all.

My father loved his kids, but he didn't have a relationship with us. He didn't know how to meet our needs emotionally. He never bonded with me as his son.

> "THIS FEAR WAS YET ANOTHER DRIVING FORCE THAT SEPARATED ME EMOTIONALLY FROM MY FATHER."

I believe the absence of a deep trust and expressed faith in God caused him to not know and not hear the inward guiding voice of the heavenly Father regarding the needs of children, which go far deeper than physical provisions. Thankfully, my father received salvation and became a believer two years before he passed away.

One of the major purposes parents have is revealing to their children the existence and presence of a Creator, a Purpose Giver, a heavenly Father. It is through relationship with our heavenly Father that we come into our purpose, gifting, destiny and reason for this earthly journey.

I believe one of the best ways to understand and value your maleness — your masculinity — is to be close to another trustworthy male. Maleness is transmitted by presence and emotional bonding, not just by verbal communication and/or physical presence alone. It is a father who reveals to his sons (and daughters) the male image of the heavenly Father. Emotional oneness with a father results in a confidence with one's identity. The absence of emotional oneness with one's father usually results in struggles with finding one's identity, which sometimes results in gender confusion and/or full acting out in homosexuality. Fear and anxiety often follow this type of identity crisis, which usually gives rise to deep-rooted anger. Lack of affirmation and connection with a same gender parent can often lead to deep latent or overt anger issues which carry over into adult relationships with hurtful and painful consequences.

> "EMOTIONAL ONENESS WITH A FATHER RESULTS IN A CONFIDENCE WITH ONE'S IDENTITY."

I now know to be created in the image of God, regardless of gender, is to be created with both masculine and feminine characteristics. I personally believe masculine and feminine attributes of God were placed into the man he created called Adam. God created Adam with masculine and feminine attributes in one body. When he saw it wasn't good for Adam, His creation, to be alone, God took out the feminine attributes of Himself and put them in a being He called woman.

We cannot believe men are *all* masculine and women are *all* feminine. Both have masculine and feminine qualities. C.S. Lewis once said, "God is so masculine, that He makes all of creation seem feminine in comparison." If you were to define masculinity in terms of the attributes of God, it would be defined as the power to initiate, which is demonstrated in the physical anatomy of a male. Femininity is the ability to receive. Jesus was the perfect balance of masculinity and femininity, because He always took initiative in the things of God, yet He was always careful to receive from the Father. He never did anything He didn't receive from the Father (John 10:17–18). Jesus was constantly receiving from the Father *and* initiating the things of God.

Because my dad was absent in his bonding with me, this is what happened in my life. I thought being a man — *being somebody* — was all about sex. My overwhelming desire throughout my childhood was to become a man, but from the very early stages of my childhood, I had some confusion. I was sensitive, tenderhearted, kind and gentle ... all traits more closely related with females.

> "I THOUGHT BEING A MAN ... WAS ALL ABOUT SEX."

Because I was stronger on the feminine side, there were times my peers at school, and even my siblings, would tease me and make me feel rejected. Although my mother always accepted me the way I was, no one, including her or my father, ever explained to me that God creates us that way as individuals.

I had no one to tell me that men can be tender and loving and caring. Those were feminine attributes that no one equated with being a man. When I discovered God had created me to be "different" and one of those differences was that I was going to be loving, sensitive and caring and that my masculinity would flow through those character qualities, I realized the image of God in me was legitimate. He had created me this way intentionally. Once I recognized God created me that way, it helped me to become comfortable with who I was as a man.

A complete person has both masculine and feminine traits, and God creates us this way as individuals. I now know the image of God is in me — the Spirit of God is on the inside of me as a man. God has put in me both masculine and feminine qualities, and He has put a creative force on the inside of me that is my will. So I have the ability to make a choice and to initiate the things of God and God's favor will be upon it.

> "A COMPLETE PERSON HAS BOTH MASCULINE AND FEMININE TRAITS, AND GOD CREATES US THIS WAY AS INDIVIDUALS."

My father was also absent when I needed to learn about sex and becoming a "man." Sex education wasn't taught in school at that time. Really, no one ever mentioned anything about sex. They would have run you out of town. I learned about sex from my best friend. We played together in the afternoons when

I was an adolescent. He didn't know any more about it than I did, but he had an older cousin who had seen pornography and shared his sexual information. That was my sexual education. As a result, my concept of being a man meant I needed to have a sexual experience. So I set out as a young teenager to try to have a sexual experience. (I didn't have sex before I was married, but it wasn't because I wasn't on the prowl. By the grace of God, nobody cooperated.)

I didn't hear about college until I went to high school. Nobody in my family had ever talked about college. My first goal was to graduate from high school. My goal after that was to go to college. I wanted to *be somebody*, and I knew college would help make that happen. So I set out to find a way to go to college.

After I finished high school, the only opportunity I had to go to college was to join the Air Force. I was going to be drafted into the armed forces anyway, so instead of being drafted into the Army, I chose the Air Force because they promised I could go to college.

My basic training took place at Lackland Air Force Base in San Antonio, Texas. Until that time, I had never left my hometown in Alabama. From there, I went to Chanute Air Force Base in Illinois for Personnel School. While there, I drew an overseas assignment to Thule Air Base in Greenland. This was my first time to leave the country.

Greenland is part of the ice cap; the dirt is permafrost, frozen year around. So here I was, living overseas and far away from home, and there were 5,000 airmen on base and virtually no females. In fact, there was a saying about this place: "There is a girl behind every tree, but there are just no trees in Thule, Greenland." And it was true. There were a couple of nurses in the hospital, but they were high-ranking officers. I was an enlisted man, and they didn't want anything to do with me. So, in a manner of speaking, there were no women in Thule.

This is where I was first introduced to pornography. I'd heard about pornography from my best friend's cousin, but this was my first time to see explicit sexual acts. Looking at pornography was fairly common among men in the service. As a result of my experience, I came back with more knowledge about life and sexuality and what I thought it meant to be a man.

When I was younger, I didn't know there were normal God-given changes coming about in my body and that I would have sexual desires and those desires were normal. No one told me the feeling and desires in my body were not bad, but good. I wish I had known all young men go through these changes and develop a sex drive. I wish I had known that although this sex drive would get very strong, I could and should set boundaries and develop self-control in managing my sexual desires. This would have greatly helped me shape my life as a real man of character able to make good choices.

"I GREW UP BELIEVING IN ORDER TO BECOME A MAN I HAD TO HAVE A SEXUAL EXPERIENCE, WHICH I NOW KNOW IS NOT TRUE AT ALL!"

Most of all, I wish I had known this God-given sex drive, as strong and dominating as it was, was not my true identity. I grew up believing in order to become a man I had to have a sexual experience, which I now know is not true at all! My sexuality was and is only a *part* of who I was and the man I was to become.

God made us sexual beings. It's normal to be sexual, but it's not our identity. The culture we live in says sex makes you a man. Therefore, if you don't have sex, you don't have an identity. The concept that you must have a sexual experience in order to be a man — in order to have character — is foreign to Scripture. Jesus Christ, the greatest man who ever lived, modeled what it was like to live in this world and not have sex. We get our true identity not from our sex drive, but from our relationship with our heavenly Father.

CHAPTER 4

I WISH I'D KNOWN HEAD KNOWLEDGE IS NOT THE SAME AS HEART KNOWLEDGE

For with the heart one believes unto righteousness, and with the mouth confession is made unto salvation. For the Scripture says, "Whoever believes on Him will not be put to shame." For "whoever calls on the name of the Lord shall be saved."

— *Romans 10:10 – 11, 13*

After I completed my service in Thule, Greenland, I came back to the US and was stationed at an Air Force base in Savannah, Georgia. Since I lived so much closer to my family in Alabama, whenever possible, I'd spend weekends visiting my mother and older brother, Max, and his family. Max, who was six years older than me, had already served in the military and was now pastoring a church in Alabama.

One Sunday during a weekend visit, I met a young lady at my brother's church. She and I soon started dating, and we fell in love. We had a whirlwind romance and, after three months of dating, we started planning our wedding. Weeks later, my brother performed our wedding ceremony in his church. I still believed the lie that in order to be a real man I had to have a sexual experience and, now that I was married, I hoped to finally feel like a "real" man.

After we got married, my wife stayed in Alabama and continued living with her parents and working for a group of attorneys while I lived back at the base in Georgia. I came to see her whenever I could, and in the meantime, we wrote letters back and forth and talked on the telephone every chance we got. It was difficult being apart, but I was determined to make it work.

> "I STILL BELIEVED THE LIE THAT IN ORDER TO BE A REAL MAN I HAD TO HAVE A SEXUAL EXPERIENCE AND, NOW THAT I WAS MARRIED, I HOPED TO FINALLY FEEL LIKE A 'REAL' MAN."

We had been married for about three months when I received an urgent call from my brother. "You need to come home. Your wife is in the hospital," he said. I came home on emergency leave to discover she was having a miscarriage. The Air Force gave me leave for a few days so I could stay with her, but it wasn't long before I had to go back to the base.

Another three months passed, and my brother called again. His tone was just as urgent as he once again said, "You need to come home."

"Is my wife in the hospital again?" I asked.

"No, just come home."

"What's the deal?" I asked, a little irritated he wouldn't tell me what was going on.

"Well," he started, "I'm your pastor. But I'm also your wife's pastor and, even though you're my brother, I can't break a confidence. But you're going to have to trust me. You *need* to come home."

"Okay." I hung up the phone not knowing why I needed to come home or what was going on.

I left as soon as I was allowed and went straight to my wife's parents' house to see her. She greeted me at the door, and we hugged. We walked into the living room and sat down on the couch. She looked at me and said, "I think I need to just tell you."

"Is something wrong?" I asked.

"Yeah, we need to talk," she responded.

"Okay."

"I don't want to be married to you," she blurted out.

"What are you talking about? I'm in love with you!"

"We made a big mistake," she continued. "I don't want to be your wife, and I'm not going to be your wife."

Stunned, I looked at her and said, "Look, I don't know what's going on here, but you just gather up your belongings because I'm taking you back with me. You're coming with me back to Savannah, and we'll work out all these details. We can't work them out with you here and me there."

"No, I'm not going," she responded.

"Yes, you are. Just pack your bags. I'll help you pack. You're going with me. You're my wife. You have to come with me," I persisted.

Once again she said, "I'm not going with you."

Desperate, I asked her, "Where are your parents?"

"I LEFT THE HOUSE THAT EVENING, AND I NEVER SAW HER AGAIN."

Her parents came in the room, and they agreed with me. They told her, "Pack your bags. You made a choice to marry Tommy, and you need to go with him. He's willing to take you, so just go on."

But she refused.

I spent the entire day trying to convince her to go with me. At the end of the day, she looked at me and said, "I am not going with you," and then she just stopped talking to me. That was the last thing she ever said to me. I left the house that evening, and I never saw her again.

I kept calling and writing her. I wrote her a letter every day begging her to come back to me, promising I'd do anything in the world to make our marriage work. Of all the things that had ever happened to me or anyone in our family, as poor as we were and as many problems as we had, divorce wasn't one of them. No one in my family had been divorced. I would be the first, and I was devastated.

My family advised me to get an annulment, but she had already processed the divorce. She arranged the divorce through the attorneys she worked for and cited abandonment as grounds. She took the responsibility for abandoning me and sent me divorce papers.

I went to my attorney and let him read the papers. He said, "She's giving you a clean slate. She's not claiming or wanting anything. She just wants out of the marriage." So I signed the papers.

I was divorced.

I was abandoned.

I was alone.

> "NO ONE IN MY FAMILY HAD BEEN DIVORCED. I WOULD BE THE FIRST, AND I WAS DEVASTATED."

I felt so much rejection, and as a result, I went back to the base and became very depressed. She had opened up old wounds and created new ones. I was devastated. I started thinking about how I ruined my life and my family's lives. Even though my family was trying to encourage me, I was so depressed it didn't help. I felt like my journey was at an end. I had finally had my sexual experience, and I still didn't feel like a man. It had done nothing but devastate me. I was done.

That's when I started planning my suicide.

I was required by the government to take out life insurance policies. I had one policy that listed my mother as the beneficiary, and I transferred the other policy I had that listed my wife over to my mother. My plan was to make my death look like an accident so that my entire insurance policy would be paid out to help my mother. That would be the end of it. No more pain, and my mother would be taken care of.

After careful consideration, I planned to drive over the Talmadge Memorial Bridge in Savannah, Georgia. This is an enormous bridge that connects South Carolina and Georgia. I was going to run my car off the bridge and end my life.

For the next few days, I drove over the bridge and mentally planned my demise. I eventually found the perfect spot and decided on the night I was going to carry out my plan.

Before the divorce and even a few times after, I had attended Ardsley Park Baptist Church in Savannah on Sundays. There were a couple of airmen I knew who also attended, but I would usually sneak up to the small balcony and sit in the back row all alone.

Whenever I did go, it was usually just so I could see Mrs. Hall, a silver-haired, Spirit-filled lady in the choir. I'm pretty sure she sang off key, but she sang with everything in her. She had the joy of the Lord like I'd never seen before. There was something about the way she sang that connected with me. She had something that I didn't have. Something I wanted.

The night arrived when I had decided to end my life. I dressed in my uniform and went out to my car at ten o'clock. As I was driving my car off the base, I looked down at the passenger seat and saw a church bulletin sitting there. I picked up the bulletin and looked at the address on it. It was the address to the pastor's house. I didn't know the pastor and had never spoken to him personally, but I decided I would go by his house before I drove over to the bridge. I reasoned that if I was going to take my life, I better be right with God.

I drove down the pastor's street and found his house. I didn't even need to look for the house number. The front window was open, and from the street I could see he was sitting inside reading his Bible. I parked my car, went to the door and rang the doorbell. He came to the door and, seeing me in my uniform, invited me in.

> "I REASONED THAT IF I WAS GOING TO TAKE MY LIFE, I BETTER BE RIGHT WITH GOD."

I told him I was planning to commit suicide that night, but I wanted to be right with God. We talked and talked, and I told him my history. I told him about how I'd been raised in church and that I had been baptized before.

Finally, he said to me, "You're a believer. I just think this circumstance with your wife and your divorce has gotten the best of you. I'll tell you what, let's settle this issue tonight. Get down on your knees."

I got down on my knees, and he knelt down there with me and said, "I want you to repeat after me. Lord, I know I'm a sinner. I know I need a Savior. I accept Jesus Christ as my Savior and Lord. Forgive me of my sins and come into my life. Amen."

When we finished praying, I got up off of my knees, and the pastor said, "Okay, I want you to write something down. Write down: 'On September 16, 1959, at 12:25 am, I prayed the sinner's prayer.'" I wrote it down on a piece of paper before I left, and he told me to go home and put it in my Bible.

"THAT NIGHT, UNBEKNOWNST TO ME, GOD TOOK EVERYTHING I'D EVER LEARNED, EVERYTHING I KNEW, OUT OF MY HEAD AND PUT IT INTO MY HEART."

It wasn't that I didn't have the understanding or the head knowledge before I met with the pastor that night. I had grown up going to a Southern Baptist church in rural Alabama. My Sunday school teacher, Mrs. Burks, taught me about Jesus and how to be saved. I had the *head* knowledge of how to be saved. I knew to confess my sin. I knew Jesus was my Savior. I knew I had to ask Him to come into my heart. But those things had to become real in my *heart*. When I met with the pastor that night, I gained a new awareness in my heart that there *is* a God; there *is* a way to salvation. That night, unbeknownst to me, God took everything I'd ever learned, everything I knew, out of my head and put it into my heart.

Before my conversion, I'd listen to a sermon and think to myself: *I know this.* And, to be honest, I did know it. After my conversion, my thoughts changed from *I know this* to *The Lord is speaking to me about how He wants to change me, and how He wants to shape my life.* That's true even today. It's not that I'm unfamiliar with the biblical content; but it's those moments when I feel internally God is doing something inside of me; He's revealing something deeper to me.

It's the difference between *seeing* something and really *hearing* something. It's the difference between knowing and *knowing.* It's knowing in the core of your being what is true.

The great danger people in churches face today is falling into the habit of going through the routine, the liturgy, without there being any substance. Often, people who attend church cannot tell you the subject of the sermon three days later. It's because they're not receiving anything that's life-changing. But then there are times we hear a message or a word during church, and we know we'll never be the same because of what we heard. It's because it's full of substance, and substance comes from the heart. It's those encounters with the Lord that are life-changing.

What's interesting is that science is now beginning to reinforce the importance of our hearts beyond a physical level. In a 2007 study by Professor Mohammed Omar Salem called "Heart, Mind and Spirit," he concludes: "It has long been thought that conscious awareness originates in the brain alone. Recent scientific studies suggest that consciousness emerges from the brain and body acting together." He goes on to say, "a growing body of evidence now suggests that the heart plays a particularly significant role in this process [of cautious awareness]. Findings indicate … the heart is more than a simple pump. In fact, it is now seen as a highly complex, self-organizing information processing centre with its own functional 'brain' that communicates with, and influences, the cranial brain via the nervous system, hormonal system and other pathways."

I've seen many star athletes and celebrities wear crosses around their necks, making sure the cross is visible for all to see. They wear it as a fashion statement, but the Bible tells us the cross is a place of death. So when a person wears a cross around his neck, it should be to declare to the world, "I'm dying to myself." But the behavior of many people who wear crosses actually shows they're not interested in dying to their own selfish desires and ambitions. To those people, Jesus would say, "your heart is far from Me" (Mark 7:5–7). You may *say* you're following God, but your heart is far from Him if you don't have the heart knowledge of what the cross means.

This lack of heart knowledge isn't limited to those outside the church either. In many seminaries, future pastors are taught everything *except* how to be a man of God. As a result, they come out of seminary with a head full of *knowledge* about the Bible, but with very little heart *understanding* of God's Word.

In Matthew 5:20, when Jesus was looking at the Scribes and Pharisees, He said to His disciples "that unless your righteousness exceeds *the righteousness* of the scribes and Pharisees, you will by no means enter the kingdom of heaven." The amazing thing about that statement is the Scribes, Pharisees and Sadducees were the most knowledgeable religious people — the theologians — of that day, yet Jesus said there was nothing in their behavior that reflected they knew God at all.

The Scribes transcribed the Scriptures by memory. They didn't have anything written down … they just remembered. They had a head full of knowledge, yet nothing was in their hearts. There are many people in the world today who have knowledge about God, but their hearts are far from Him. That could be said of me in my own journey. During my teenage years, I was elected to be the church clerk. As an officer of the church, I recorded all the historical records of the church by taking notes during business meetings and other church events. I was active in my church and knew all that was going on, but I didn't have a relationship with Jesus. All I had was head knowledge about God.

> "THERE ARE MANY PEOPLE IN THE WORLD TODAY WHO HAVE KNOWLEDGE ABOUT GOD, BUT THEIR HEARTS ARE FAR FROM HIM."

I now understand that head knowledge is not the same as heart knowledge. When I left the pastor's house that night, I didn't feel any different. I was still depressed. I was still numb. My emotions and feelings didn't seem to have changed at all, but I decided to go back to the base and not follow through with my plan.

It was one o'clock in the morning by the time I got back to my barracks, so I went straight to bed. I woke up later that morning, got dressed and went into the office. A friend of mine who worked in the maintenance squadron called to ask if we could get together for lunch at the chow hall.

As I walked down the road on my way to the chow hall, he walked toward me and called out, "Hey Tom! What happened to you?"

"What are you talking about?"

"You look different," he said.

"*What* are you talking about?" I asked again as he drew closer.

"You're different. There's *something* different about you," he said as he continued looking at me with wonder. "What happened?"

"I accepted Jesus last night," I said.

"Man! Did you ever! Come on, tell me about it!"

"EVERYTHING ABOUT
ME HAD CHANGED."

We walked into the chow hall and found a table away from everyone else where we could talk. I told him what had been going on in my life, about the divorce, the planned suicide, meeting with the pastor and my salvation experience the night before. After I finished talking, he said, "You know when I asked you what happened? I could tell something had changed. You always walk with your head down. You're almost always slumped over. Today, when you were walking toward me, your head was up and your back was straight, and you actually smiled! It's been a long time since I've seen you smile!"

I hadn't even realized I was smiling, but I couldn't stop. Everything about me *had* changed. My countenance, my thoughts, my entire life. After I came to *know* the Lord in my heart, I never had another suicidal thought again.

+ CHAPTER 5 +

I WISH I'D KNOWN TITLE AND POSITION ARE NOT AS IMPORTANT AS MINISTERING IN MY GIFTING

Don't think you are better than you really are. Be honest in your evaluation of yourselves, measuring yourselves by the faith God has given us.

▶ Romans 12:3 (NLT)

Shortly after my conversion, I began to feel the Lord calling me to ministry. By this time, I was attending Ardsley Park Baptist Church on a regular basis. One Wednesday night, the pastor preached about surrendering your life to ministry. (He actually preached on that subject quite often, and many of my fellow airmen went into ministry as a result of his teaching.) At the end of the sermon, I walked down the aisle, crying like a baby and met the pastor at the altar.

"I've been feeling this pull toward ministry," I told him. "I stayed up all night trying to settle this issue with the Lord, but I can't refuse Him anymore. I surrender."

It was obvious to him I was being called to serve the Lord, so he encouraged me to go to college and seminary. Since I was already in my third year of a four-year term in the Air Force, I immediately began submitting college applications to Christian universities.

But there was one obstacle I had to get through. It was the 1960s, and Baptist universities didn't accept divorced individuals as ministerial students. So I prayed about it and said to the Lord, "If You're really in this — if You're really calling me to ministry — I want to do it the right way, which means I need to attend a Baptist or Bible college."

> "GOD HAD CALLED ME TO MINISTRY, AND I BELIEVED HE WAS GOING TO PROVIDE FOR ME."

I wrote to every Baptist college in the country trying to get accepted as a student on a ministerial scholarship. I had money from the G.I. Bill, and I also received many private contributions to my education from friends.

Some of the people who gave the money wanted to remain anonymous, and to this day I still don't know who they are. God had called me to ministry, and I believed He was going to provide for me. Those anonymous contributions to my college fund are absolute proof that He did.

After weeks and months of waiting, I finally heard back from Howard College (now Samford University) in Birmingham, Alabama. It wasn't an acceptance letter, but it was the closest thing I'd received so far. The letter said that if I could get three people who knew the circumstances of my divorce to share what they knew and if their stories were the same as mine, they would present my application before the board and they *might* accept me.

As quickly as I could, I asked three people to write letters on my behalf. They each wrote to the university letting them know my divorce wasn't due to any fault on my part and that I was willing to work for the marriage, but my wife was not. I still remember the day I got the letter in the mail from Howard College saying the board had accepted me. It was one of those pivotal moments in my life I'll never forget. I could really feel God at work. I really *knew* He was there.

While I was applying to universities and finishing my last year of service in the Air Force, I also started serving during Christian Youth Hour at the church. We had about 200 students who would come every Saturday night for youth service.

Shortly after I started serving, I became president of the Christian Youth Hour and preached my first sermon. It wasn't long before I started preaching on a regular basis. I didn't know much about the Bible, but I was always studying and would just preach what I knew.

Not only was I getting my first pastoral training from Ardsley Park Baptist Church, but I also met a young college student there named Nancy. At the time, Nancy was attending Armstrong Junior College in Savannah, Georgia, and was also the pastor's secretary. Because she was there every time I'd come to see him, she knew my story. Despite my past, I could tell she wanted to be a friend to me. The problem was I had completely sworn off women. I'd had my sexual experience, and I'd been rejected. Bitterness had filled my heart. In fact, I'd half seriously told the Lord, "I'll just become a Catholic priest. That way, I'll never have to worry about marriage again!"

There was only one problem with that. Something had happened in my heart. The Lord had become personal to me and, as a result, He was already working behind the scenes to reorganize and restructure my life. And it all began when I met Nancy right after my salvation experience.

"ALTHOUGH I'D SWORN OFF WOMEN, I COULDN'T HELP FEELING ATTRACTED TO HER, EVEN AS A FRIEND."

We became good friends from the very start. Although I'd sworn off women, I couldn't help feeling attracted to her, even as a friend. Because Nancy was six feet tall, she and I could actually have eye-to-eye conversations. We just enjoyed being around one another from the very beginning. That friendship was orchestrated by the Lord to meet this deep longing in my heart for friends and an even deeper longing (that I didn't even realize I had) to be friends with women.

At the same time, our growing friendship was meeting a need in Nancy's life. She would call me at the base on behalf of the pastor to check up on how I was doing and ask if I was going to be at church on Sunday. She did all the things a pastor's assistant does, but I now see it was also her way of being my friend and reaching out to me. I also see that the Lord was working through her to put my life back together and to begin the process of me being able to carry out His will in my life.

I had been licensed by the church to preach and, a few weeks before I left for college, the pastor gave me a printed license to take with me. Nancy was in charge of typing the licenses and signing her signature along with the pastor's signature. When the pastor handed it to me, Nancy turned to me and, quoting the book of Ruth, said, "Whither thou goest, I will go," and pointed to her signature.

Later she asked me, "If I write to you when you're away at college, will you write back?" I said, "Maybe." And I was true to my word. She wrote me quite often and, occasionally, I'd answer her.

While I was in college, I started working the night shift at the Birmingham Trust National Bank. I would go to school all day, and then go in to work at ten o'clock at night. My job was to sort checks by hand. Each person on the shift had a section of the alphabet, and we worked three or four hours a night. Sometimes on holiday weekends, I wouldn't get home until two or three in the morning.

A few years into college, I ran out of money and didn't have enough to continue my education. I decided to drop out of school and apply for a full-time job at the bank in installment loans. I went in and talked with Guy Caffee, the Vice President of Installment Loans and a graduate of Howard College. He decided to create a job just for me so I could continue going to college. He worked it out so I could go to college in the morning and work in the afternoons, evenings and weekends.

I scheduled all my classes for the morning and went to work each day at noon. Part of my job was to repossess cars, and there were days I would drive all over the state of Alabama and not get home until nine o'clock at night. More often than not, my responsibilities on the weekends included flying to different states to restructure loans and, if needed, retrieve cars. I'd get on an airplane on Friday night and if we couldn't rework the payment plan, I'd drive the repossessed car back to Birmingham, getting home by Sunday evening.

Occasionally, I'd get weekend assignments in Atlanta. By this time, Nancy had accepted a job with the Georgia Baptist Convention and was living in Atlanta. So whenever I was in town, I'd call Nancy and we'd go out to dinner. Then I'd finish working the account and go back home.

Even though it was never for very long, it was always nice to see her. She was always so friendly, and we enjoyed one another's fellowship. One time she came to visit me in Birmingham, and I took her with me to visit my mother in Montgomery. All the while, we were just good friends.

About my third year in college, I began to get really lonely. One day, I was talking very frankly to God about my feelings. I grumbled, "Lord, I guess I'm really going to be a bachelor for the rest of my life. But Lord, I'm a male, and I need companionship."

The Lord revealed to me that I had been driven to get married the first time based on my desire to be somebody. Then the Lord said to me, "I've had a wife for you all along. You never had a wife; you had a sexual experience that was legal. If you want her, you'll have to go get her."

I knew He meant Nancy.

I called my mother and said, "You know that girl who came with me to see you three or four months ago? I think the Lord is saying I'm supposed to marry her." With my mother's blessing, I decided to pursue Nancy.

I wanted to see her as soon as possible, but she was serving as a counselor at a summer camp in north Georgia for several weeks. I eventually got an assignment from the bank to take care of business in Tennessee, which just so happened to be near the camp where Nancy was working.

I made arrangements to meet her one evening in the cafeteria. We had dinner together and then took a walk around the camp. Once she had shown me all the sights, I finally mustered up the courage to say, "I think the Lord said we were supposed to be together."

"I've known that since the day you left for college. I've just been waiting on you."

Then I kissed her for the first time.

My proposal wasn't traditional, but it was all that needed to be said between the two of us. I didn't have enough money to buy an engagement ring, and she said she was okay with that. We got married on March 20, 1964, and exchanged wedding bands. Years later, I was finally able to buy her a diamond ring.

I'd carried around the burden about my past for so long, but my past wasn't even on Nancy's radar screen. She knew every sordid detail, but to her it was like it had never happened. She never once brought it up. Over the years, when I would get down on myself or

> **"SHE KNEW EVERY SORDID DETAIL, BUT TO HER IT WAS LIKE IT HAD NEVER HAPPENED."**

feel inadequate in ministry and start talking about things I did wrong, she wouldn't go there with me. She never brought it up or used it against me. It just wasn't an issue. It was settled in her heart before we even got married.

(Not too many years ago, before she passed away, Nancy and I took a trip and returned to the very same spot on the campground where I proposed, and we kissed again.)

A year after we got married, I graduated from college. (It took me five years to get my four-year degree, but I finally had it!) I was still working for Birmingham Trust, but had been offered the pastorate at a church. The day I went in to quit my job, Mr. Caffee called me into his office.

"Tommy, do you remember the day I gave you this job?"

I said, "Yes, sir."

"Today I want to offer you a permanent job. I think I know the answer to this, but I'm going to ask you anyway. You're one of our top collectors and now a college graduate. If you'll stay with the bank, I'll double your salary. Will you accept a full-time position?"

"Mr. Caffee, thank you, but I can't," I responded without any hesitation.

"I know that. I know there's a ministry call on your life, but I had to offer it to you just to see if you wanted it."

> "IF YOU'LL STAY WITH THE BANK, I'LL DOUBLE YOUR SALARY."

Just the fact that he offered me the job showed me how valued I was. I'll always be indebted to Guy Caffee. He gave me a job that allowed me to finish school and still make a decent living.

Two years after I started pastoring a church, Nancy and I moved to New Orleans, Louisiana, and I enrolled in New Orleans Baptist Theological Seminary. I also worked in the campus store on weekdays between classes.

I eventually became the store manager on a profit sharing program and pastored a church on the weekends. After I graduated from seminary, I moved to Jasper, Alabama, and became the Senior Pastor at New Prospect Baptist Church.

A few years passed, and I increasingly became very unsettled in my spirit. There was an emptiness on the inside of me that caused me to begin examining my calling and all the work I'd put into getting my formal education. I had worked so hard to get through high school, college and, ultimately, seminary. But now that I had finally arrived, I discovered I was as empty as I could be. More than ten years of my life had been devoted to study and preparation for pastoring, yet it had come to feel more like a regular job than a calling. I still liked what I was doing, but there wasn't a lot of joy in it. It began to feel tedious and laborious. It felt like something was missing.

> "MORE THAN TEN YEARS OF MY LIFE HAD BEEN DEVOTED TO STUDY AND PREPARATION FOR PASTORING, YET IT HAD COME TO FEEL MORE LIKE A REGULAR JOB THAN A CALLING."

One night, as I was preparing the Sunday message in my study, I began talking to the Lord about how I was feeling. I'd heard that Billy Graham lays down prostrate before the Lord, and I thought it would be a good thing for me to do too. As I laid down flat out on the floor of my study, praying and talking to God about my life, I looked up on the wall and noticed my degrees. I'd amassed quite a collection, including my high school diploma, my ministerial license, my bachelor's degree from Howard College and my master's degree in theology. I was *really* proud of my accomplishments.

I realized I had reached the goal I'd set long before to get my degrees and become somebody. Having my degrees and the title and position of pastor was important to me. I was proud to tell people I was a pastor, because I had now arrived at the place where I knew what it took to be one. Many churches would only consider pastors with seminary degrees, and because of that, titles and degrees were important in the position of "pastor."

That night, I told the Lord, "If this is all there is to being a pastor, I'm going to get a different job! I'm going to find a good job, and I'm going to be a good Christian, but I'm leaving the ministry."

And the Lord answered me, saying, "You've assumed that because you have all your degrees and you know about Me that you *know* Me. But *knowing* Me is totally different and has nothing to do with your position or your title. I'd like to offer you the opportunity to get to *know* Me."

I said, "Lord I *want* to know You!"

"WHAT I CAME TO REALIZE IS MY DEGREES, MY TITLE, MY POSITION—NONE OF THEM—MEANT A THING"

What I came to realize is my degrees, my title, my position — none of them — meant a thing if I didn't have the character and relationship with my heavenly Father to go with it.

It wasn't just about my degrees and accolades; it was about my experience and relationship with God that made me different from being a run-of-the-mill pastor. I discovered it was much more important to God that I minister in my gifting.

That night, God began taking me on a journey where I discovered I wasn't called primarily to be a senior pastor. God had instead given me gifts in other areas. The Holy Spirit began moving in me and drawing me to Himself to fill the emptiness on the inside of my soul. I began really zeroing in on what my gifting was. Although I was still in a pastoral role, I came to learn there was a calling on my life to become a "visionary," a pastor with a vision for the work of the Lord in a given area. I knew what it was like to love people, to minister to their needs and to preach the Word, but I never had a vision of where a church ought to go. During this season of my life, I began doing away with my title as senior pastor and the position of being the "head guy." I began to look internally at what God wanted to do *in* me, which started a healing process with the Lord working things *out* of me.

Many, many years after that night in my study, I met a man in Texas by the name of Milt Green. Milt had only finished the seventh grade and had no other formal education, yet He was the most versed man of the Bible I have ever known. He was a carpet cleaner by trade, and, once while he was cleaning carpets, the Lord began to speak to him: "You see this dirt that you're getting up out of the carpet? I want to get that out of your life also."

Milt began to read the Bible as much as he could. He'd start early in the morning and read until late into the evening, stopping for a bit to talk about what he read. Sometimes he would get to a word he couldn't pronounce and he'd just say "hard word" and skip over it. What he created by his reverence, respect and understanding of the Word of God was an atmosphere for the Holy Spirit to reside. It's what I now call a "Word atmosphere." Milt had no formal training whatsoever, yet it was he who led Evangelist James Robison through the process of freedom and healing. He was just operating in his gifting, and God did the rest.

Milt wasn't created to be a carpet cleaner; that was just what he did in order to be able to pay the bills. He was created to lead others to freedom and healing through Jesus Christ. Like Milt, when God gives you your gifting, it doesn't really matter what your title is for you to operate in that gifting. I now know the gifting of God that He's called us to do seldom has anything to do with a position or a title.

CHAPTER 6

I WISH I'D KNOWN THE HOLY SPIRIT IS A GIFT, NOT A DOCTRINE

"So I say to you, ask, and it will be given to you; seek, and you will find; knock, and it will be opened to you. For everyone who asks receives, and he who seeks finds, and to him who knocks it will be opened. If a son asks for bread from any father among you, will he give him a stone? Or if he asks for a fish, will he give him a serpent instead of a fish? Or if he asks for an egg, will he offer him a scorpion? If you then, being evil, know how to give good gifts to your children, how much more will your heavenly Father give the Holy Spirit to those who ask Him!"

≈ Luke 11:9–13

Just two Sundays after I prayed and told the Lord I wanted to know more about Him, I went into my study to get ready and wait until the morning worship service began. I always prided myself on the way I went in to the worship center and made my appearance shortly after the service began. After all, they taught us in seminary when the senior pastor, "the man of God," enters the worship center, whether preaching or just participating, the eyes of the congregation should be on him. It was my practice to stay in my study and pray until the congregation began singing the first song, and then I would make my appearance.

There was always a point in every service when I would lead the congregation in a pastoral prayer. I would first make myself a list of all the people who I knew were sick. Then, when it came time to do the prayer, I'd call them by name, pray for the service, the congregation and any other issues that needed prayer. I was very thorough, and I was intentional about not missing a name or a need.

On this particular Sunday morning, I entered the worship center, walked across the platform and sat down in one of the two big throne-like chairs facing the congregation. I stood up to do the pastoral prayer, and as I was walking between my chair and the pulpit, my knees buckled, causing me to instantly drop. Unable to get up, I prayed on my knees publicly for the first time in my life. I didn't pray my prepared list; I just prayed what was on my heart. At that moment, something in me broke, and my journey with the Holy Spirit began.

> "AT THAT MOMENT, SOMETHING IN ME BROKE, AND MY JOURNEY WITH THE HOLY SPIRIT BEGAN."

There was a little old lady in my church (every church has a little old lady) who would always make it her business to encourage me after each service. About three weeks after my knees buckled, she came up to me and got as close as she could.

"What's going on with you?" she asked.

"I don't know, but the Lord is doing something inside of me," I responded.

"Yes, He is, and I can tell you when it started!"

"When?" I asked.

"The morning your knees buckled," she said matter-of-factly. And she was absolutely right.

God had done a work in me. He was in the process of breaking everything in me, yet there was peace in my soul. Even though I'd told the Lord I was ready to leave the ministry, my heart had changed. I was having an encounter with God and experiencing the move of the Holy Spirit in my life. I was getting to really *know* Him. Now, I never wanted to leave New Prospect Baptist Church. I was ready to be there for the rest of my life.

Out of nowhere, I started receiving letters, packages and magazines in the mail I hadn't subscribed to or that weren't even addressed to me. They were either put in my mailbox with somebody else's name on them or dropped off at the church office by people I didn't know.

And they all had a similar theme … they all contained information about different aspects of the Holy Spirit. I started reading these materials and studying about encounters people had with the Holy Spirit in the Bible. As a result, the Lord began teaching me about Himself and things of the Holy Spirit I'd never been exposed to before.

Some men from the local Assembly of God church came to see me one day during the week while I was in my study. They knocked on my door and asked if they could meet with me. We went up to my office and once we got situated, one of the men said to me, "I heard you got the Holy Ghost."

"Well, I know that something's going on in my life that has never happened before, and I'm one of the happiest men I know anywhere," I said.

The man replied: "I have come to meet with you, because the Lord sent me here to teach you how to speak in tongues."

Taken aback, I responded, "I appreciate you and understand you're following your heart and what you think you heard the Lord say, but I'm not going to let you teach me to speak in tongues."

> "I HAVE COME TO MEET WITH YOU, BECAUSE THE LORD SENT ME HERE TO TEACH YOU HOW TO SPEAK IN TONGUES."

The man said, "Well, when you get ready, let me know, because I can teach you."

"Well, I will. Thank you so much. I appreciate your friendship and appreciate you praying for me."

While I didn't speak in tongues that day, the visit from those men was confirmation of what the Lord was doing in my life. Over the next twelve months, I began to experience a liberty and freedom in my soul that started to manifest through my ministry. I began to see people from a different perspective. They didn't irritate me as much, and I started loving them more. I was no longer dissatisfied with the pastorate. Pastoring became a joy again and was no longer just a job. I could sense my calling more than ever and knew I was doing exactly what the Lord had called me to do.

Up until this point, I'd gone all my life with an incorrect understanding of what God's Word says about the Holy Spirit. Based on studying about the Holy Spirit, in both college and seminary, I had concluded the Holy Spirit was sent just to validate the person of Jesus Christ. But in the Bible, Jesus plainly says the Holy Spirit is a gift.

In Luke 11:9–13, Jesus said:

> "So I say to you, ask, and it will be given to you; seek, and you will find; knock, and it will be opened to you. For everyone who asks receives, and he who seeks finds, and to him who knocks it will be opened. If a son asks for bread from any father among you, will he give him a stone? Or if he asks for a fish, will he give him a serpent instead of a fish? Or if he asks for an egg, will he offer him a scorpion? If you then, being evil, know how to give good gifts to your children, how much more will your heavenly Father give the Holy Spirit to those who ask Him!"

In this passage, Jesus was explaining how ridiculous it is to assume the Holy Spirit is not a good gift. Our heavenly Father, who knows all and is totally good in all of His actions, would *never* give His children a gift that wasn't good, a gift that wasn't important. And as His children, we should receive His gift — the gift of the Holy Spirit.

There are many divisions in the body of Christ over what it means to have the Holy Spirit. On one extreme, there are those who feel that unless you're dancing in the aisles, standing on pews, shouting from the pulpit and having an emotional experience, you couldn't possibly be in the Spirit. The other side of this extreme says the Holy Spirit is a part of the Trinity but has no part in life today. Some have even made a doctrine out of who has the gifts and who doesn't have the gifts, what the gifts are and what they are not or if the gifts are intended for this time of our lives or for another time. Admittedly, it's not so much the Holy Spirit who's controversial as it is the *gifts* of the Spirit. But why do we let the manifestations of the Holy Spirit — the gifts — keep us from walking in the power of the Holy Spirit? The biblical truth is God's Word says the Holy Spirit is a gift to *all* believers. The early disciples were told to wait for the coming of the Holy Spirit because that's when and how they would receive power. This gift from God for all believers is the enabling power of God through the Holy Spirit to accomplish His will and purpose for our lives.

"BASED ON STUDYING ABOUT THE HOLY SPIRIT ... I HAD CONCLUDED THE HOLY SPIRIT WAS SENT JUST TO VALIDATE THE PERSON OF JESUS CHRIST."

Many pastors who do the work of the Lord know what to do in terms of pastoring a church, but the life of God as it's expressed in the Holy Spirit is absent in their lives. It's all the work of man. But God gave us a gift to enable us to accomplish His purposes — the gift of the Holy Spirit.

In the church where I grew up and in the seminary I attended, the Holy Spirit was reduced to what happens to you when you're born again. The Holy Spirit does a work in your heart to bring you to Christ. This and this alone was believed to be the work of the Holy Spirit. I now know God gave us the gift of the Holy Spirit to empower us to be filled with His love and His power to accomplish His will in our lives. The difference is there is an infilling, or a baptism, of the Holy Spirit, that goes beyond the salvation experience. All believers can experience it, but it has to be received by faith. And when I received the gift of the Holy Spirit, I reached a whole new plateau in my life. My pastor, Robert Morris, explains it this way: God the Father baptizes you in Jesus, His disciples baptize in water, and Jesus comes and baptizes us in the Holy Spirit.

Just as I was starting to embrace my calling, I received a phone call that changed the course of my life. I was in my office at the church studying for the Sunday message when the phone rang.

"Hi! I'm Norma Baxter. I live in Fort Worth, Texas, and I want to know if you're preaching on Sunday?" she quickly blurted out.

"Yes," I said, "but if you're part of a pulpit committee, I want you to know I'm not interested."

"I understand," she persisted, "but are you going to be preaching on Sunday?"

After assuring her I'd be preaching and making sure she understood I wasn't interested in leaving my church, I hung up the phone. That following Sunday, a group of five people showed up. They tried to spread out across the congregation as if they were hiding, but that was impossible to do in our small family church. Everybody knew everybody; they could have had a sign in front of them that said, "We're not from here!" and they wouldn't have stood out any more. After the service, some members of my congregation told them to stay away from their pastor. They made it clear that if the visitors were after their preacher, he was *not* available.

I met with them a few hours later that afternoon. They told me they were indeed a search committee and began telling me about their beautiful church. An architect in their church had designed it and it was a very modern-looking structure with a slanted roof and a bell tower. All of the features inside and out were updated and modern. The pastorium was a beautiful house with four bedrooms, three bathrooms and a double car garage. Everything from the church to the pastorium was so much nicer than anything we'd ever had before. Yet even though they were trying to persuade me by telling me how wonderful everything was, I told them I really wasn't interested. I was happy where I was. I was finally settled in my soul. I'd gone through a difficult season, but the Holy Spirit was doing such an incredible work in my life, I wanted to stay right where I was.

"I WAS HAPPY WHERE I WAS. I WAS FINALLY SETTLED IN MY SOUL."

They said they understood and left for Texas. Or so I thought.

The next morning, I was leaving the church to go preach at the Walker County Pastors' Conference, and as I was pulling out of the driveway, their car pulled in. I could see them frantically waving at me, so I rolled down my window.

"We'd like to talk to you again," they said.

"I'm sorry, I don't have time to talk to you right now. I'm going to preach."

"We understand, but when will you be through?"

"I'll be back at the church around 12:30 pm."

"Okay, we'll meet you here at 12:30 pm," they said.

Unbeknownst to me, while I was preaching, they went downtown and asked the people at the bank and in the stores about my reputation. After I finished the conference, I met with them and they said, "We want you to know we stayed in Birmingham last night, and we prayed together. It's unanimous. We believe you're supposed to be our next pastor."

I'd been to Texas a few times in my life — when I was in the Air Force and when I worked for Birmingham Trust National Bank — but I never dreamed of pastoring a church in Texas. Never! I mean that was so far away from my thoughts. I never even considered it.

Before I could answer, they asked, "Would you be willing to come out and preach for us one Sunday? Then, will you pray about whether or not you should be our pastor?"

Reluctantly I said, "Okay, I will."

A few weeks later, the search committee flew me out to Texas. They showed me the church and the beautiful pastorium. Everything was just as they had described. I preached on both Sunday morning and Sunday night. Before I left on Monday, I went to the church and prayed behind the pulpit. That's when I felt like the Lord told me, "This is your new assignment."

I went home and told Nancy about my weekend. "I let them know I'm not sure what I'm going to do, but I feel like the Lord is saying something to me about this place. They want to bring me back, and they want you to come with me."

I flew back to Texas, this time taking Nancy with me. We spent the weekend seeing the area, and I preached twice on Sunday. They were careful to make sure Nancy saw the pastorium. We'd never lived in a house that big. Every time I prayed, I heard the Lord say, "This is your new assignment."

They flew me back out a third time, and this time I told them I would accept the call if they issued one. They voted me in that night. I went back to Alabama, resigned from New Prospect, and moved my family to Haltom City, Texas.

"EVERY TIME I PRAYED, I HEARD THE LORD SAY, 'THIS IS YOUR NEW ASSIGNMENT.'"

A few years after moving to Texas, a deacon in my church introduced me to his brother, Cecil McGee. Cecil lived in Titusville, Florida, and attended Peter Lord's church. The church campus had a retreat center just for pastors, and Cecil invited Nancy and me to an all-expenses-paid retreat.

This was the first Spirit-filled Baptist church I'd ever been to in my life. Unlike churches I'd gone to or pastored, this church was actively involved in worship. They weren't just a church that sang three stanzas of a hymn and that was the extent of their worship. They were people who acted as though they really understood the words they were singing. And they were expressing themselves by lifting their hands to the Lord in praise and worship! They were hugging one another and even shouting to the Lord occasionally. There was such joy and peace as they worshipped; it was unlike *anything* I'd ever experienced. And all this was happening in a Baptist church!

Through this church, the Lord had orchestrated a perfect way for me to be exposed to the Holy Spirit within the context of my upbringing and the denomination I'd given my life to. I was exposed to things of the Spirit and the Spirit of the Lord working in the lives of people and expressing Himself. I saw joy, peace, goodness, faithfulness and gentleness. For the first time in my life, I saw the fruit of the Spirit (Galatians 5:22–25) manifested in the faces and actions of people. I returned to Texas with a hunger to be like that. It was a major step in my journey in learning about the Holy Spirit.

During the retreat, the Lord really dealt with my heart. They asked the pastors there to make a "sin list" of all the things in our lives that were not of God. They then took us through a prayer of confession, and I experienced true freedom for the first time in my life! It was awesome!

I came home from that pastor's retreat a completely different person. I was getting to know the Holy Spirit in a way I'd never known Him before. I was beginning to learn to hear His voice and obey His promptings.

After I came home, I became very conscious of the fact that although I had shared about my divorce with the pulpit committee before I accepted the pastorate in Haltom City, I had never shared it publicly with the church. The pulpit committee had chosen to make it a closed issue and said it wouldn't affect my call because they believed God said I was supposed to be their pastor. But when I came back from our retreat in Florida, I felt like I was supposed to tell my story to the entire congregation.

The very next Sunday, I stood in front of the congregation and said, "I'm not going to preach a normal sermon today. I want to share something very personal with you."

I went on to share with them all the details of my life. I told them I had been divorced before I met Nancy, and that my family knew, including my children, but the church at large did not. Knowing the stances and the convictions many Baptists have about divorce, I explained I was convicted that past week and didn't want to continue as their pastor under

"FOR THE FIRST TIME IN MY LIFE, I SAW THE FRUIT OF THE SPIRIT ..."

false pretenses. I shared my whole story. I shared about how I came to know the Lord after my divorce and how I surrendered my life to be in ministry. I wanted the entire church to know all there was about me.

As a symbolic gesture at the close of the message, I took out the keys to my car and my house and I laid them down on the Lord's Supper table. (At the time, I was driving a church-owned car and living in a church-owned house. My total income — everything we had — was from the church.) They were symbols of my releasing back to them what they had given me as their pastor.

I said, "As of this morning, I'm no longer your pastor. I would like to continue as your pastor, but I'll only be your pastor if you call me in light of the story I have told you this morning. I'm through covering up any part of my life from this day forward. I cannot live without you knowing who I am."

One of the deacons stood up and said, "I make a motion that we go into a business meeting." The motion was immediately seconded, and the congregation voted to go straight into a business session. They presented me as their pastor, and the congregation voted unanimously to call me their pastor. That day, I experienced *complete* freedom like never before.

A few years later, I went with my youth group to Falls Creek Assembly in Oklahoma, and Jack Taylor was preaching on the subject of walking on the water. I heard the Lord say, "I want to teach you to walk on water. I want you to resign your church."

> "I WANT TO TEACH YOU TO WALK ON WATER. I WANT YOU TO RESIGN YOUR CHURCH."

I went home and told Nancy, "Honey, I think the Lord is saying our time at Haltom Road is over."

"What are we going to do? Are you being called to another church?" she asked.

"No. But I feel like I'm supposed to resign."

"He hasn't told *me* that," she responded.

I went back to my study and said to the Lord, "Lord, funny thing … you know the woman you gave me? She didn't hear what I heard."

I heard the Lord say, "Wait on her." And I waited one solid year.

I did everything I knew to lead the church into being a Spirit-led church. I'd always heard that if you're leading and you turn around and nobody is following, you're just taking a walk. During that time, I would turn around and see nice people who loved me, but nobody was really following me. As a church, they chose to remain true to their Baptist beliefs about the Holy Spirit.

One Sunday after church, Nancy and I were sitting at the table eating lunch. I had just delivered what I thought was the best sermon I'd ever preached and Nancy turned to me and said, "Do you still feel we should leave the church?"

"Yeah, I do."

"I'm ready," she said. And I resigned the next Sunday.

CHAPTER 7

I WISH I'D KNOWN
FAITH WAS THE KEY TO MY DESTINY

But without faith, it is impossible to please Him; for He who comes to God must believe that He is, and that He is a rewarder of those who diligently seek Him.

➤ *Hebrews 11:6*

The Sunday before I resigned from Haltom Road Baptist Church, I was having lunch at the Chicken Shack and met a man by the name of Bill James who owned a custom drapery manufacturing business. After I resigned, Nancy suggested I call him to see if he had a job available. She knew I would need to do something until the Lord told us what He was going to do with us, since my entire income had come from the church and we didn't have any savings. Our kids were in Christian school, and we had to move out of the pastorium into an apartment and give back the church-owned car. I had no way of providing for my family at all. I was beginning to learn what it was like to walk on water.

I found the phone number for James Contract Draperies and called him up. "Mr. James, I met you a couple of Sundays ago," I said. "I just resigned as pastor of Haltom Road Baptist Church."

"I know who you are!" he said.

"I would like to come and talk to you about a job," I continued.

"Come on!" he said.

I left the house the next day and drove 20 minutes to meet Bill at his office. The family-owned drapery factory was located on Raider Drive in Euless, Texas. Along with the executive offices, it contained a long, rectangular sewing room with 75 sewing machines, a cutting room filled with

> "I WAS BEGINNING TO LEARN WHAT IT WAS LIKE TO WALK ON WATER."

all different sizes of folding tables and cutting boards, a huge warehouse stacked with fabric from floor to ceiling, a room just for making drapery rods and a shipping department with a dock in the back. The building was massive!

I walked in the front of the building where the executive offices were, and Bill's secretary showed me to his office. I told him my story and asked if he had something I could do that would help me provide for my family until I found out what the Lord wanted me to do next. After hearing me out, he asked me when I wanted to start.

"Well, a week from now would be good," I said.

"Come on! I've got a job for you."

From my interview, I determined the company's primary purpose was to manufacture draperies for hotels around the country. Other than that, I didn't know much about what I'd be doing or how much money I'd be making. Even so, I *knew* this was my next step.

I also didn't know I'd be working in a hot warehouse sorting and organizing fabric all day! It was the middle of the summer, and the warehouse was the only part of the building that didn't have air conditioning. It was hotter than blue blazes! And there was fabric all over the place! Piles and piles of cloth just stacked everywhere without any

> **"I NOW KNEW WHAT I'D BE DOING. AND I WASN'T TOO EXCITED ABOUT IT."**

organization. On my first day, Bill walked me to the warehouse and said, "I need this warehouse straightened out, and you're in charge." I now knew what I'd be doing. And I wasn't too excited about it.

As I soon learned, it became my job to look at the orders, determine whose material we should use and pull the fabric that went through the sewing assembly line to make the drapes. I was the starting point for an order, so everything had to be very organized.

One week I was pastoring a church and sitting behind a desk each day preparing for the Sunday message, and the next week I was sweating my butt off in a huge warehouse moving cloth around and getting it organized. It nearly killed me. But God had told me it was time to walk on water.

For six months, I worked in the grueling heat of the warehouse, all the while talking, praying and, frankly, complaining to the Lord. And I didn't hear *anything* from Him. There was no change in my situation. There was no answer. I was hot, miserable and frustrated. And I was stuck.

On one particularly hot summer day, after I got everything in the warehouse organized, I sat down and wiped the sweat from my brow. Miserable and exhausted from the heat and backbreaking work, I grumbled out loud to the Lord, "Boy, this is the pits! Here I am with a master's degree. I'm the most educated man in the whole company. And I'm working in a warehouse, the lowest job in

"IN RESPONSE, THE LORD WAS SILENT."

the company! Lord, I thought when You were going to teach me to walk on water, I was going to move into another phase of ministry. I want to know where my ministry is! Where is it? What is it? This is *not* what I thought was going to happen!" In response, the Lord was silent.

A couple of days after my rant, I woke up in the middle of the night and heard the Lord say, "You asked Me about your ministry."

Fully awake after hearing that question, I responded, "Yes, Lord!" I was starting to feel excited! *Okay, this is it! He's going to reveal to me where I'm going!*

Then I heard Him say: "If the teachings, the sermons and the truths you know about the Word of God and which you've proclaimed to others don't work in your life in this place where I have you now, don't bother teaching them anymore. That's your new assignment."

He had *finally* answered me and that's what He had to say ... *the warehouse was my assignment?!* But I knew He was right. I had to accept that for now my ministry was in the marketplace.

A few more weeks passed. I was in the warehouse organizing fabric when I heard Bill call me on the intercom: "Tommy, come up to my office!"

I went to his office, and he looked at me and bluntly said, "I think it's about time I told you something."

"What is that?"

"Remember the day you called me for a job?"

"Yes, sir. I do."

He said, "That morning in my prayer time, I asked God to send me someone to help me with this company. When you walked through the door, I felt like you were the man. But first I had to find out if you would work." He continued, "I now know you will work. You've proven that in the warehouse. Today I want to offer you a position in this company. I want you to be the Director of Operations. You'll answer to me and me alone."

"Wait, wait, wait! I'm in ministry — I'm *called* to ministry," I protested.

"Tommy, I know that."

"Well, I may not be here very long," I blurted out.

"I know that too. But as long as you're here, will you take the job and help me?" he asked.

"Bill, I don't know how to make drapes," I responded honestly.

"*I* know how to make drapes, Tommy. I just want *you* to help me manage people."

I left his office not knowing what my answer would be. Later that night, I went home and told Nancy what Bill said. Without hesitation, she said, "Sounds good to me!"

The next day, I accepted the position. I was furnished with a van to drive and was put on salary. For the next six years, I oversaw daily operations and more than 100 employees of this multimillion dollar company. I also took every opportunity to preach at different local churches on weekends.

During this time, we lived in an apartment, but our three children were growing quickly and we needed more space. Nancy started shopping around for houses and found one in Haltom City. The price was right, but the thought of buying a house scared me to death! I knew I could afford the payments with the money I was making at James Contract Draperies, but I had never owned a piece of property. In fact, my dad had never owned a piece of property—ever! This was all new to me. Not having a father to turn to for wisdom and direction, I went to Bill for advice.

"There's this house in Haltom City. This is the price, and here's what the payments would be each month," I explained. "I know I can get it financed, and I have money for the down payment. I just don't know if I should do it or not."

Bill looked me straight in the eye and said, "Tommy, for goodness' sake, buy the house!"

So I did. And for the first time in my life, I owned a home. It was a huge step of faith, and it was all a part of the process of learning how to walk on water.

"I HEARD THE LORD SAY, 'OKAY, IT'S TIME FOR YOU TO LEAVE.'"

By this time, I had settled into my job working for Bill. In fact, he'd become a mentor to me and was one of my dearest friends. The kids were doing well in school, we were able to pay all our bills, and the truck I drove to work was provided for by the company. Life was good. I was content. Then one day at work, I heard the Lord say, "Okay, it's time for you to leave."

Later that night, I went home and told Nancy I felt like the Lord said it was time for me to leave my job. It was time to move on. This time her response wasn't as positive. "Okay, but I don't think *I've* heard that," she said.

I protested, knowing I had heard clearly from the Lord. "I don't think so," she continued. "We're doing better financially than we've ever done, and you're preaching and teaching almost every weekend. We're in ministry *and* you're making a living. I like it. It's okay with me if things stay like they are."

And she was right; we were doing great financially, much better than we did when I was in the pastorate. I told her I'd pray about it further, but I still felt in my heart I was supposed to leave. I knew there was something the Lord was pulling me toward.

One morning, shortly after my conversation with Nancy, Bill took me out to breakfast. Going to breakfast with Bill wasn't all that unusual; in fact, we went out to breakfast quite often. I'd come in the office at six-thirty in the morning and get

> **"I NEED TO CUT BACK 25 PEOPLE, AND I NEED TO ELIMINATE YOUR POSITION."**

things going. Once I made sure everyone was at work and the orders were moving ahead, Bill and I would often step out for breakfast. So I had no reason to think things would be any different this particular morning.

Once we were seated and the waitress had brought our food, Bill looked at me and just started crying. "Tommy, I've got to do something that is the hardest thing I've ever done in my life," he said. "I'm going to have to let you go. I need to cut back 25 people, and I need to eliminate your position."

"It's fine," I said. "The Lord told me three months ago I was supposed to leave the company, and I couldn't bring myself to do it. Most of the people you're going to lay off have been hired by me, so allow me to lay them off. And don't tell anyone in the company I'm leaving until I get all the layoffs done. Let me do that for you. Once that's done, you can announce to the company that I'm also leaving."

He looked at me with an expression of shock and asked, "You want to do that?"

"Yeah, I do. I *want* to do that for you," I replied.

"Okay. That's the way we'll do it."

He thought I was going to be upset, but I wasn't. I was relieved. I didn't know what I was going to do next, but I knew I'd heard the Lord's voice, and I was at peace with the decision.

That next Sunday, I went to preach at Cross Timbers, a non-denominational church in Valley View, Texas. For a while, I'd been commuting back and forth each weekend to preach there as an interim pastor. It was my way of staying connected to ministry, and it helped fill the vacancy in the pulpit. Before I stepped up to preach, I let one of the elders know my job was being eliminated. He responded by saying, "That's really interesting, because the elders met this week and voted to bring you on as our pastor. We'd like to offer you a full-time position."

I *knew* that was the Lord. I went back to work on Monday and told Bill I was going to be the pastor at Cross Timbers. My family and I were going to be okay. With my salary and the job Nancy got working at the kids' school, we'd make enough to pay for the house and other expenses. It was my first pastorate outside of the Southern Baptist denomination. I had no idea that would end up being my last pastorate as senior pastor.

When I took the warehouse job, I didn't think there was any way I'd be there more than six weeks. And when I became the Director of Operations, it had already been six months. I ended up staying with the company just under seven years.

During this time in my life, I discovered that walking on water would involve coming to the place in my journey where I was willing to trust God completely with my family, my needs, my income — *everything*. There was no backup plan. No other options. I had to *choose* to believe God and His promises, even when I didn't know the plan. I learned to trust Him even when I didn't know the next step.

> "I HAD NO IDEA THAT WOULD END UP BEING MY LAST PASTORATE AS SENIOR PASTOR."

Faith is a gift of God, but it isn't automatic. You have to initiate faith in times of doubt and disappointment. The root of the word "faith" means "to lean toward; to rely on; to trust." Just like the time I was working at the warehouse, there are still times when I pray and don't get an answer. But those are the times I have to initiate my gift of faith; I have to lean toward, rely on and trust God to meet all my needs.

Faith is a choice. We have to *choose* to believe. When we're faced with circumstances in our lives, we have to make a choice to exercise the faith that is in us. Our heavenly Father holds our destiny and our reason for being here. He knows what part we have in the work of His kingdom. We just have to choose to believe and trust Him even when we can't hear Him speaking.

Faith in God is a major key to living a fulfilling and rewarding life. My destiny — my purpose in life — is tied to my trusting and believing God for myself. My personal faith in God is the key to being fulfilled, happy and living in peace throughout my whole life.

The times when I pray and don't get an answer, when I look everywhere and cannot and do not see the Lord, when I search the Word of God and receive no revelation, when I search for light and find darkness … *those* are the times I have to choose to operate my gift of faith. I have to choose, at that moment, to use the gift of faith God has put in me. And what I've discovered is when my faith goes to work and I'm worshipping the Lord and surrounding myself with other believers, I don't have worry. I just have to trust God and walk in peace knowing He's going to do what's best for me.

"FAITH IS A CHOICE."

In the early days I was simply taught (what I heard was) in order not to go to hell you have to have faith in Jesus. You have to believe in the Lord Jesus Christ (which is absolutely true). But no one ever told me that having faith in Jesus was a key to life. As you trust the Lord, He opens up your horizons, your future, to give you a vision of who you are and where you're going — what your purpose is. I lived a great portion of my life just stumbling through. Then I began to realize that as I express faith in the Lord Jesus Christ, I get revelation about life. I get understanding and wisdom about life. Now I see in the distance where I'm going with my life ... I see what this journey is all about.

It's something I constantly have to remind myself of. After Nancy went to be with the Lord, I became lonely and began questioning God. Nancy had suggested I should get married again — she actually gave me permission — and I was praying about what I should do. I wanted the Lord to tell me if I was supposed to get married again or not. I kept praying and asking God, but I didn't seem to get any answers at all. In fact, there were times I would pray and I couldn't hear anything. I would get in the Word and cry out to God, but there was no response; I wasn't hearing anything from the Lord. It was a *really* dark time.

One night, I woke up in the middle of the night and couldn't go back to sleep. All of these feelings and emotions were crowding in on me. I was all alone in an empty house, and I called out to the Lord, "I don't understand why You don't make it perfectly clear *exactly* what I'm to do."

And the Lord said, "I *am* making it perfectly clear. I want you to trust Me and exercise your faith. I have your best interests in mind, and I'll let you know about things as you need to know them."

Faith is the best gift when you don't get answers. It's God's way of asking us, "If I don't give you what you ask for, will you trust Me?"

"I WOULD ... CRY OUT TO GOD, BUT THERE WAS NO RESPONSE"

✣ CHAPTER 8 ✣

I WISH I'D KNOWN
THE POWER OF INTERCESSION

Therefore I exalt first of all that supplications, prayers, and intercessions and giving of thanks be made for all men.

➤ 1 Timothy 2:1

After I left home and went into the service, I would come home on leave to visit my mother who was living alone in an apartment in Montgomery, Alabama. She knew I'd be driving in late at night from Hunter Air Force Base in Savannah, Georgia, so she'd stay up praying for my safety. When I'd come in, sometimes well after midnight, I'd see her sitting in her easy chair, sound asleep, with her open Bible laying across her chest. My mother believed in the power of prayer and intercession, and there were many times across the years she went to sleep praying and interceding for me.

When I was a young boy, not even old enough to go to school, a circuit preacher by the name of John Lofton would come stay in our home whenever he was in our part of the country. He was a black man who would walk across the country going from one community to another preaching and proclaiming the gospel. Even though we were poverty stricken, my mother made sure whenever he came through town, we'd have a place for him to sleep and food for him to eat. Because of his color, this was virtually unheard of in southern Alabama at the time.

My mother always asked John to pray over her children before he left. One time in particular, I was lying on a pallet on the floor, and before he left our house, he knelt down and laid his hands on me and prayed for me and my brothers and sister. I can still remember him putting his big, black lips on my cheek and kissing me, loving on me and blessing me. I believe that, through John, God removed all prejudice from my heart. God imparted to me that He is not a respecter of persons; that people are just people. The color of a man's skin, his educational level, his economic status ... none of that is important. A person's

"GOD IMPARTED TO ME THAT ... PEOPLE ARE JUST PEOPLE."

relationship with God is what's important. I also believe God used John to instill in me a love for Africa. In fact, I have spent more time on the continent of Africa than any other foreign region in the world.

My mother was a *great* example of what it meant to be an intercessor. I was reminded of this one morning when I dropped our kids off at elementary school. Suddenly a great fear came over me that something would happen to them. As a young father, I was deeply concerned for the safety of my children. The fear I felt was overwhelming.

After I dropped them off, I went to the church. It was still early in the morning and no one was there, so I went into the worship center, sat down behind the pulpit and just started talking out loud to the Lord. He reminded me that as a young man I hadn't given much thought, if any, to the idea that one day I would be a father and have children of my own. As I pondered this, I said to the Lord, "You're absolutely right. I never dreamed I would have children and would be a father. It never crossed my mind. I'm not sure what I was thinking about, but I never thought about having a family. It's almost like I woke up, and all of a sudden I had three children."

I went on to tell the Lord I didn't think I deserved my children, I didn't feel like I was a good father, and I didn't feel worthy of them. Then I thanked Him, saying, "Your goodness to me is overwhelming, because even though I didn't put any thought into having children, I deeply love them."

As I was meditating and praying, the Lord said to me, "Son, I know your feelings." (Whenever the Lord talks to me and uses the word "son," it's always an endearing term; it draws my heart to the heart of the Father.) He said, "Son, I know your feelings about your children, but you had a praying mother who interceded for you. I'm the one who made you a father and chose to bless you with three children. As a matter of fact, you're in the ministry because she interceded for you and I had to answer her prayer."

At that moment, I understood and comprehended that God answers prayers of intercession.

There's a story in the Bible that beautifully explains the power of intercession. In the book of 2 Chronicles, you can read about the story of Jehoshaphat, the King of Judah, who reigned over Judah for 25 years. He was responsible for bringing reform back to Judah and reestablishing a complete commitment and trust in the Lord for the tribe of Judah. Then the people of Moab and the people of Ammon rose up to come against Jehoshaphat and the people of God. Because Jehoshaphat was very much afraid, he "set himself to seek the Lord, and proclaimed a fast throughout all Judah. So Judah gathered together to ask help from the Lord; and from all the cities of Judah they came to seek the Lord" (2 Chronicles 20:3–4).

Jehoshaphat went into the temple before the Lord and called out to God and reminded Him that He was the God of the fathers of Israel and Judah, and of all the kingdoms of the earth. He gave credit to God for who He is, and he reminded God the temple had been built on His behalf. In other words, Jehoshaphat came before God with an attitude of intercession on behalf of His people. He reminded the Lord about how in the past He hadn't allowed the children of Israel to destroy the people of Moab, Ammon and Mount Seir and all the people who were now coming up against them. He then said, "O our God, will You not judge them? For we have no power against this great multitude that is coming against us; nor do we know what to do, but our eyes are upon You" (2 Chronicles 20:12). And they stood before the Lord and waited. It's a magnificent picture of the king of Judah standing and interceding on behalf of the people of God.

"Then the Spirit of the Lord came upon Jahaziel ... And he said, 'Listen, all you of Judah and you inhabitants of Jerusalem, and you, King Jehoshaphat! Thus says the Lord to you: "Do not be afraid nor dismayed because of this great multitude, for the battle is not yours, but God's. Tomorrow go down against them. They will surely come up by the Ascent of Ziz, and you will find them at the end of the brook before the Wilderness of Jeruel. You will not need to fight in this battle. Position yourselves, stand still and see the salvation of the Lord, who is with you, O Judah and Jerusalem!" Do not fear or be dismayed; tomorrow go out against them, for the Lord is with you'" (2 Chronicles 20:14–17). As a result of Jehoshaphat interceding, the Spirit of the Lord responded and reminded him he wasn't going to have to fight this battle. All he had to do was show up. The Lord was going to fight this battle for them. It's one of the greatest stories about the power of intercession.

> "THE LORD WAS GOING TO FIGHT THIS BATTLE FOR THEM."

Somehow in my journey with the Lord, no one had ever told me I could stand in the presence of God and intercede according to the will of God on behalf of my battles. I now do that on behalf of my children, my grandchildren and anything that concerns me.

It's a life-changing principle I wish I'd known earlier in my life. There are so many times I would have come before God, laid my burdens upon the Lord and waited for Him to give me answers.

The Lord has used prayer and intercession in other ways in my life. As I mentioned previously, I used to be frightened by the spiritual world, that unseen reality. This world we live in is *not* the real world. It's simply where life takes place. I've also learned there's an unseen world, and sometimes the Lord pulls back the veil and gives you a glimpse of what's to come.

While I was pastoring at Cross Timbers Church, Nancy and I became good friends with Don and Sherry Fox. After we left Cross Timbers, Sherry was diagnosed with cancer and battled the disease for several years. Nancy and I would visit her in the hospital and spend time praying for her healing and interceding on her behalf. Her family really believed they had received a word from the Lord that she would be healed, and they asked everyone they knew — her children, relatives, friends and pastors — to stand with them and pray for her healing.

After a long fight, Sherry passed away.

Before the funeral, Don called and asked if I would come and visit with his family at Cross Timbers who were gathering at the church to pray. They had decided to bring Sherry's body into the worship center so we could pray for her to be resurrected. I told them I would meet them there and we could pray together.

We started asking for the Lord to resurrect her, praying: "Lord, we know You've done this before, and we believe You can do it for Sherry." Suddenly, I felt compelled to lie down on the floor behind the pulpit, and as I was praying, I heard, "I do not want to come back." It was Sherry's voice! At first, I thought she'd been resurrected, but then I realized the voice I heard wasn't coming from her body. I jumped up off the floor and ran over to where Don and the other family members were sitting.

"Don," I said, "I just heard Sherry say she didn't want to come back."

He just looked at me with shock on his face and said, "I heard that too, but I thought it was just me."

"You really heard it?!" I asked, amazed.

"Absolutely."

"Okay, let's stop this thing."

> "I MISSED HER TERRIBLY AND FELT SO ALONE. I WAS FULL OF SELF-PITY."

We announced to the family what we had heard and that we believed we heard Sherry saying she did not want to come back. So we stopped praying for her resurrection, but our hearts were encouraged because the Lord had allowed us to have a momentary encounter with the heavenly realm.

Just a couple of years ago, my wife, Nancy, passed away after a long battle with colon cancer. Not too long after, I was walking through the house and having one of my grieving moments. I missed her terribly and felt so alone. I was full of self-pity. Out of nowhere, I heard clearly in my mind, "Your wife is having the time of her life!"

All of a sudden, my attitude changed. I realized I could grieve, but I wasn't going to mope around and wish I had her back. Tears are given to us for a reason; they wash our souls. They're our way of emotionally and physically letting grief drip off of us. It's okay to cry when you have losses, as long as crying doesn't become something you make yourself go to because it's your comfort zone. The Enemy will use our grief to steal our time here on earth from doing things we should be doing by distracting us with the pain of our loss. Pretty soon grief can control you and you can go into introspection as well as self-pity and miss the reality of the day the Lord has given you. All the while, the one you're grieving for is having the time of their life. I now know interceding brings protection, direction and freedom for me … and for others.

CHAPTER 9

I WISH I'D KNOWN IT IS POSSIBLE TO LIVE IN FREEDOM

"And you shall know the truth, and the truth shall make you free."

✣ *John 8:32*

Nancy and I left Cross Timbers Church in 1987, and I went on staff with James Robison at Life Outreach International (formerly James Robison Evangelistic Association). Although my freedom process began at the pastors' retreat in Titusville, Florida, it really progressed when I came into relationship with James Robison and Milt Green. Yet, I didn't realize how much bondage I'd been in until I went on staff at Restoration Church in Euless, Texas, in 1989. During this time, I experienced freedom in a whole new way.

In the early 90s, there was an event going on in the Vineyard Church in Toronto, Canada, which became known as the "Toronto Blessing." It was a movement of God like nothing I'd ever experienced or heard of before. Our senior pastor, Doug White, decided he wanted all of his pastoral staff to go to Toronto and participate in what the Lord was doing. So that our work at the church wouldn't be hindered by our absence, he decided it was best for us to go up there in couples, two at a time, for a week. When it came time for us to go, Nancy and I were joined by Pastor Mark and Sandy Jobe.

I was *very* skeptical about what was taking place in Toronto, because the atmosphere was totally different from anything I'd ever known before, including my Titusville experience. I'd heard about all the people who were being touched by the Lord and experiencing manifestations, but I was doubtful this was truly a work of the Lord.

"I WAS DOUBTFUL THIS WAS TRULY A WORK OF THE LORD."

The very first service we went to changed my unbelief into belief.

The service began with a time of teaching and went into a prayer time. At the end of the service, people lined up for personal prayer. As each one got to the front of the line, the leaders would touch them on the forehead. Many would fall on the floor, while some would break out in uncontrollable laughter. Some would scream. Others would start dancing. It was weird; yet, at the same time there was something so unique about the people I observed … they were truly free! They didn't care what other people thought about them. There was an element of freedom I'd never seen before. The ideals I grew up with — being proper, dressing well, looking good and praying right — were just thrown out the window. The people looked like they were enjoying the Lord … and they were!

I finally decided to let somebody pray for me. I got up and went to the back of the prayer line. In the depth of my being, I reasoned within myself that if the person tried to push me or force anything on me, I would resist. I would push back. It wasn't long before it was my turn. The man who was going to pray for me just touched me on the forehead; it was no more than half a second, and then he just moved on. I didn't *feel* anything. I didn't fall out. I didn't laugh. I didn't cry. I didn't *do* anything. There was absolutely no emotion expressed. There was nothing I could sense about how I felt that was any different. I walked back to my seat and sat down by my Nancy and that was it … until three o'clock in the morning.

We all went back to the hotel, and Nancy and I went to bed. At three o'clock in the morning, I woke up shaking uncontrollably.

> "*I DIDN'T FEEL ANYTHING … THERE WAS ABSOLUTELY NO EMOTION EXPRESSED.*"

95

It was almost like I was having a chill, but I wasn't cold or uncomfortable; I was just shaking uncontrollably all over. Then I saw something; it came through the window into my bedroom and then into me and then back out the window. I was shaking so violently, I was afraid I was going to wake up my wife, so I got up and went into the bathroom. Suddenly, I started laughing, and I could not stop. The harder I tried to control my shaking and my laughing, the worse it got. I could not control it. I went back into the room and sat in a chair across from the bed. As I was still shaking and laughing hysterically, Nancy woke up from all the commotion and asked me what on earth was wrong.

"I have no idea what is happening, but I cannot stop shaking and laughing," I said through the laughter.

"Well, I'm trying to get some sleep, so could you keep it down?"

I put my clothes on, went out in the hallway and called Mark. He said he'd come meet me in the hallway, and when he saw me, *he* started laughing and shaking. There we were, two grown men, down on the floor in the hallway of our hotel laughing and shaking uncontrollably.

When I later asked the Lord about that experience, I felt like He revealed to me why this needed to happen. I had been stuck in tradition and my concepts of what the Lord came to do for me. As a result, the experience of His presence in my body manifested itself in such a way that I had to be out of control in

**"I HAD BEEN STUCK
IN TRADITION."**

order to understand what it meant for Him to be in control. I believe He was speaking to me through that method, so I would know there are times when I can be so free in the Lord that I'm not in control of myself.

I've had several encounters like this one across the years. I don't have them as often as I once did, but out of those experiences, I've learned to walk in freedom. I wouldn't change those experiences for anything in the world, because the end result is each time I've fallen more and more in love with the Lord Jesus Christ.

There's a freedom God gives us that cannot be compared to any intellectual knowledge. It can't be compared to the normal, religious methods we use. The work of God in your heart — in the very core of your being — is unexplainable, but it is absolutely awesome and freeing!

Beyond the salvation experience, and even beyond the baptism of the Holy Spirit, is the overall principle that what Jesus did on the cross was for the purpose of setting people free. He said, "And you shall know the truth, and the truth shall make you free" (John 8:32).

The Israelites, who had been in bondage most of their existence on the earth and were in bondage to Rome even as Jesus spoke, declared: "We are Abraham's descendants and have never been in bondage to anyone" (John 8:33). That statement is characteristic of a good segment of Christians today; particularly in the Bible Belt where people attend church services every weekend and yet

"THE WORK OF GOD IN YOUR HEART... IS ABSOLUTELY AWESOME AND FREEING!"

are in bondage to sin. They've settled in on the overall thought that this is the way life is and it will never be any different. Some might say, "My mom was always like this or my dad was like this and now I'm like this. There just seems to be no help." But quite the opposite is true! Jesus came so those who would believe in Him and apply the work of the cross to their personal life could walk and live in freedom. John 8:34–36 says, "Most assuredly, I say to you, whoever commits sin is a slave of sin. And a slave does not abide in the house forever, but a son abides forever. Therefore if the Son makes you free, you shall be free indeed."

Does that mean we're sinless? No, but it *does* mean the power of sin has no control or power over us. Freedom is extremely important to the Christian life. In my own journey, as I applied the work of the cross to my personal bondages, there was a freedom that came to me. I can now live my life as a free man.

The Lord has brought freedom to so many areas of my life, including healing me from painful memories. In 2011, I spoke at a huge pastors' conference in Nairobi, Kenya, with Ronnie Matheny. There were more than 5,000 pastors in attendance. One symbol of authority in Kenya is for a man to wear a suit, including a coat and tie. Ronnie spoke before me, and he talked to the pastors about how outward appearance doesn't make a man; it's the inner heart. When it was my turn to get up and teach, I started out by saying, "Pastor Matheny said these ties we all have on are not really important. But what he didn't do is pull off his tie." And I reached up, pulled off my tie and threw it out in the congregation. Before I knew it, all 5,000 of them were

> "BEFORE I KNEW IT, ALL 5,000 OF THEM WERE PULLING OFF THEIR TIES AND THROWING THEM IN THE AIR."

pulling off their ties and throwing them in the air. Ties were going everywhere! Everyone got a new tie! The place just went bananas, and we all laughed and laughed! There was so much freedom in that moment.

A few weeks after I returned, I was facilitating KAIROS, a freedom ministry event, at Gateway Church. During one of the sessions, Pastor Linda Godsey was teaching about healing memories when a painful memory from seventh grade came to my mind.

I have always had trouble with enunciation and was never given any guidance in speech or taught how to pronounce words properly. In the seventh grade, I gave my first book report on *Bambi*. It was my first year in high school, and I was really nervous. I stood up in front of the class and began reading my book report. I pronounced the title of the book *Biambi* (Be-Am-Be) instead of *Bambi*. The *entire* class laughed. Even my teacher laughed. It was devastating. I didn't even know what I'd done wrong. I thought I was pronouncing it correctly. I had no idea why they were all laughing at me.

Over the years, that memory would come up and bring heartache and pain. Now here at KAIROS, it was coming up again. But I had just returned from Africa where I'd spoken in front of 5,000 pastors and leaders and encouraged them to literally pull off their ties as a symbol of freedom. Then I heard the Lord say, "Who's laughing now?" And instantly my memory was healed. The pain was completely gone. There is no more association with hurt when I think back to seventh grade.

We have now been doing KAIROS events for more than six years and have seen thousands of people come with heavy burdens and beaten down with bondage — even pastors and ministry leaders. Ministry has caused them to live under the burden of trying to do the work of the Lord. We have seen people come in with sad countenances and without hope, and during the course of being in the presence of the Lord, we have seen them leave full of joy and with hope! In fact, there is a progression of freedom that comes as KAIROS begins and moves through the two days. As freedom pastors, we see the bondage dropping off people as they experience the presence of the Lord and allow the Holy Spirit to do the work He wants to do in their lives.

As I look back over my personal journey out of denominational life and into a non-denominational life, I can sense the freedom that is now producing fruit in other people's lives. If I'd understood and experienced freedom as a young man, I believe I could have been bearing fruit earlier in my life.

I now know what it means to be free and that "where the Spirit of the Lord is, there is freedom." (2 Corinthians 3:17, NIV). In KAIROS, we often say that freedom is not the absence of something; it the presence of Someone. When people come to these events, we see the Lord show up and free people from their bondage.

The power of knowing you can walk in freedom and knowing there is a freedom beyond salvation is life-changing. Positionally, God sets us free from the bondage of our sin, but we live in a fleshly body, and this body is prone to be subject to the power of previous sin, areas where we have been sinned against and present tiredness and weariness ... even in the work of the Lord. If you don't know how to get free from the influence of sin in your own life, the answer is to get in the presence of the Lord and allow His Spirit to saturate your very being.

You certainly don't have to go to an event or have a Toronto-type experience to be free, but I can honestly say that because of my experiences in Titusville, Toronto and KAIROS, that I'm more in love with Jesus now than I've ever been before.

CHAPTER 10

I WISH I'D KNOWN
THE POWER OF ENCOURAGEMENT

[We] sent Timothy, our brother and minister of God, and
our fellow laborer in the gospel of Christ, to establish you and
encourage you concerning your faith ....

◆ 1 Thessalonians 3:2

Growing up, I didn't receive a lot of encouragement from my father about who I was or about the giftings that were within me. It wasn't that he didn't love me or didn't want to see me succeed; he just didn't encourage me in who I was. However, I believe the Lord placed some very specific people in my life to encourage me and whose words helped shape me into the man I am today.

When I was in the first grade, my older brother, Woody, and his father-in-law, Mr. Eiland, were visiting our house one day. I was playing in the backyard while the adults were sitting around a washpot boiling peanuts. Mr. Eiland walked over to where I was playing, put his hand on my head and said, "Tommy boy, you're gonna be somebody someday!"

His words soared through my soul. I believed what he said. It was as though he deposited the words directly into my heart. I knew one day I was gonna be somebody!

The encouragement I received from Mr. Eiland stayed with me throughout my life. It was one of the major motivations for me to work through every hardship I had along the way. It helped me finish high school, college and seminary. I believe this one statement, this one encouragement, was vital to the developmental years of my life.

In my senior year of high school, I was elected class president. That year, our senior class sponsor was Miss Evelyn Turner. She was a single lady and the type of woman who did everything "proper." Her hair was neatly cut and her clothes were always in style … she

"I KNEW ONE DAY I WAS GONNA BE SOMEBODY!"

just had everything in order. When she walked down the hall, it was as though she was walking on her tiptoes. She was a real looker. (If I were in high school today, I'd say she was hot!) And on top of all that, she was a really nice lady.

One day after school, I was sitting in the local drugstore drinking a Coke, and Miss Turner came in and sat down beside me.

"Tommy, are you aware there are several girls in the senior class who would like to go out with you?" she asked as I sipped my Coke.

"What?!?!"

Seeing she got my attention, she continued, "I didn't think you were aware of this. As your senior class sponsor, I just wanted to let you know there are several girls who have their eye on you."

I'd never dated anyone. I couldn't believe what she was saying.

She went on to say, "You don't realize that you're gifted; you're really talented. You have a great personality, and you express yourself well. I hope you can go to college."

I couldn't believe it. She had deliberately come in, sat down beside me, talked to me and encouraged me in such a sweet and kind way. She thought I could *be somebody*, that I had something in me that was good. In essence, she said to me, "You're college material." No one had *ever* said that to me! And to be honest, I'd never even thought about myself in that light.

As I've said before, my goal in life was to graduate from high school, and when I got in high school, my goal was to go to college. Miss Turner is one of the people who encouraged me to continue my education. She let me know there were possibilities out there for me.

Years later, as a ministerial student in college, I took a speech course. I knew if I wanted to be a pastor, I needed all the help I could get. My speech teacher, Mr. Guy Youmans, assigned our first speech, which was supposed to be funny. I don't remember what I talked about, but I distinctly remember Mr. Youmans sitting in the back of the classroom and laughing at my stories. His response to my humor really encouraged me to know I could be funny. He instilled in me the belief that I have a sense of humor that just comes naturally.

To top it all off, I actually got an A+ in his course. My very first speech course! It was so encouraging! I felt like I could speak in front of anybody! To this day, I believe my humor comes out of the encouragement I got in Mr. Youmans' class.

My college guidance professor, Dr. Sigurd Bryan, also served as a great encouragement to me. I was working full-time for Birmingham Trust National Bank and attending Howard College. Dr. Bryan was also my Old Testament professor. One day, I went in to see him because I was making Cs. All through high school, I was on the honor roll and made all As and Bs. I had been in the Honor Society in high school, and I'd done well in the Air Force, but I couldn't figure out why my grades were so low now that I was in college.

So one day, I went in to talk with Dr. Bryan about how I could improve my grades. "I just don't understand why I'm having such a hard time in college," I lamented.

"Tommy, how many hours are you working a week?" he asked.

"Forty to fifty," I replied.

"And you're going to college full-time?"

"Yes, sir, I'm taking sixteen hours."

"Tommy, your Cs *are* As, son. Don't ever worry again about having a C in any of the courses you take while you're working 50 hours a week. The guys who are making straight As have parents paying their way, and they don't have to work a single hour of the week. They have more time to study than you do."

Mr. Eiland, Miss Turner, Mr. Youmans and Dr. Bryan are examples in my own life of when the Lord was speaking to me through people. It was *His* encouragement that came through these voices. God used them to speak into my life, encourage me and pull out of me that which He wanted. He wanted me to become the man *He* wanted me to become, and He used other people to help me get there.

"IT WAS HIS ENCOURAGEMENT THAT CAME THROUGH THESE VOICES."

There's a great biblical example of how God can use another person to encourage others to bring about His purposes. In 1 Thessalonians 3:1–5, Paul says: "Therefore, when we could no longer endure it, we thought it good to be left in Athens alone, and sent Timothy, our brother and minister of God, and our fellow laborer in the gospel of Christ, to establish you and encourage you concerning your faith, that no one should be shaken by these afflictions; for you yourselves know that we are appointed to this. For, in fact, we told you before when we were with you that we would suffer tribulation, just as it happened, and you know. For this reason, when I could no longer endure it, I sent to know your faith, lest by some means the tempter had tempted you, and our labor might be in vain."

Paul was saying he had sent Timothy to establish the believers in Thessalonica. He then went on to say the reason he sent Timothy was to be sure the people didn't become discouraged by Paul's afflictions and the hard time he was going through. He didn't want them to become discouraged because of his hard times. But notice, in the middle of this, he sent Timothy to encourage them. Paul acknowledged that Christians are called for that very purpose. We are going to suffer tribulation, and when it comes, we need to be ready.

That's exactly what God did in my life. At the time, I didn't know God was sending these people in my life for this reason. I thought it was just circumstance. I know now God sends people into our lives at

> **"WE ARE GOING TO SUFFER TRIBULATION, AND WHEN IT COMES, WE NEED TO BE READY."**

key points to encourage us; especially when we're down and don't know what to do or where to turn. I now know to listen for the voice of God coming through the people around me and through the relationships I have.

Recently, I was at a gathering of men whom I've hunted with over the years. One cool evening after the sun had gone down, we sat around a campfire, talking and sharing stories. One of the men came over to me and said, "Man, I'm so glad you're here, because I've wanted to talk to you!" He went on to say, "About 14 or 15 years ago, you were on a hunting trip with me, and you shared about your grandson, Adam, who had passed away from cancer. When you finished sharing, I went into the other room, got on my knees and asked the Lord Jesus Christ to come into my heart. I've *always* wanted to tell you that."

It was such an encouragement that after all those years he remembered what I had spoken about and he took the time to tell me the impact it had on his life. It was another example of how God sends people into our lives to encourage us. It's like getting love letters from God.

The Bible says encouragement is the root of prophecy. As believers, we're to exhort one another with words of prophecy; with words of encouragement. Not too many years ago, I wrote thank you letters to Miss Turner and Mr. Youmans.

"AS BELIEVERS, WE'RE TO EXHORT ONE ANOTHER WITH WORDS OF PROPHECY; WITH WORDS OF ENCOURAGEMENT."

I told them, "I'm sure you won't remember me, because you taught thousands and thousands of students, but I want to let you know I went on to finish college and seminary. I'm now a pastor, and I travel all over the world preaching the gospel. I wanted you to know you had a major part in my journey. I will never forget you."

If you have the gift of encouragement or feel impressed to talk to someone about the difference they've made in your life, don't wait. Connect with that person today. More than likely, you're being used by God to bring encouragement in that person's life.

CHAPTER 11

I WISH I'D KNOWN ANCESTRAL BONDAGE IS REAL AND CAN BE HEALED THROUGH THE WORK OF THE CROSS

"The Lord, the Lord God, merciful and gracious, longsuffering, and abounding in goodness and truth, keeping mercy for thousands, forgiving iniquity and transgression and sin, by no means clearing the guilty, visiting the iniquity of the fathers upon the children and the children's children to the third and the fourth generation."

⋆ Exodus 34:6–7

I am convinced the God of the Bible is the only true God. He is sovereign. There are other false gods, but there is only one God in total control. Everything that happens to me and other believers filters through His hands. The Bible reveals God to be good and all of His purposes are redemptive.

As believers, we live under the accomplished effect, power and privilege of the cross of Jesus Christ, God's Son. Therefore, I am convinced the work of the cross has defeated the power of sin. In other words, there is absolutely *nothing* the cross does not redeem. Consequently, sins we've committed, sins that have been committed by others toward us (or done to us) and sins our forefathers have passed on to us have *all* been taken care of in the work of the cross.

Since the foregoing is true, the cross of Jesus Christ is the sole source of recovery, healing and restoration for all of our sin. This is true in my own life, but it didn't become truly real for me until I was a pastor.

When I entered the ministry after college and seminary, I began to discover passages in Scripture about the sins of the forefathers and generational iniquity. I realized the Briggs family line had ancestral bondage in the areas of intellectual, spiritual and economic poverty. Intellectually, I was the first Briggs boy by name who, to my knowledge, ever finished high school. Spiritually, very few of my ancestors were committed believers, including

"I REALIZED THE BRIGGS FAMILY LINE HAD ANCESTRAL BONDAGE IN THE AREAS OF INTELLECTUAL, SPIRITUAL AND ECONOMIC POVERTY."

my father who wasn't a committed believer until two years before he passed away. (By committed believer, I mean they were active in church life.) Economically, neither my father nor his father ever owned property or had much money.

Granddaddy Briggs passed away at our house when I was a young boy. He was in his late 80s, and his entire belongings — *everything he owned* — was in one piece of luggage. As I got older, I realized my father did the same thing in a different way. He worked on the farm his entire life and had no savings whatsoever. I then began to realize that was the case in my own life. It seemed like the family "discussions" my wife and I had throughout our marriage were always over money.

For the first 16 years of my life, we didn't have indoor plumbing or running water in our house. In order to take baths, we had to draw water out of a well and fill a huge washtub, which we'd leave outside in the sun all day to warm the water. If it was cold outside, we'd boil the water on the stove before taking our bath. Then at night, we'd take the tub in a little shelter we had outside of our house and take our baths. If we wanted to take a shower, we had another tub that had holes punched in it that we used as a shower. My brother would dip water out of the washtub and pour it into the tub with holes and it would drain down on me. That was the only kind of shower I knew until I was a senior in high school.

We lived in such poverty that if my mother hadn't been working in a local factory and I hadn't been working while I was in high school, we wouldn't have had any money to bury my father when he passed away. That's how poor we were.

After coming to this awareness, I called my older brother, Max, who was also a pastor, and discussed these thoughts with him over the phone. Once I explained to him the patterns I'd discovered in our family line, my brother said, "Oh, that has to be of the Lord! It's absolutely true. I can tell you more stories."

He began to tell me about something that happened with my dad when I was a little boy. As I've mentioned, my dad was a sharecropper all of his life. For many years, he farmed a hundred acres of land for a family. Since he didn't own the land, at the end of the year, the produce would go to pay for the use of the land, and we would take the rest. Most of the time that meant 60/40: 60% for the use of the land and 40% for our living expenses. My family did all the work of raising and harvesting the crops on the land, but we didn't reap the benefits.

Max went on to tell me about one fall day when we were harvesting the crops and the landowner came to our house. He said to my dad, "You have been faithful to us for all these years, and we would like to help you. We want to sell you the hundred acres of land you've been farming all these years. We'll let you pay as much as you can every year until you get it paid out."

My dad thought about it for a week, and he went back to the man and told him he didn't feel like he could ever pay for it. They weren't going to charge him interest; they were simply *giving* him the land and letting him pay it out as he could. But he didn't want to do it. I now believe he was bound by the spirit of poverty, and it had been passed down for generations.

> "I NOW BELIEVE HE WAS BOUND BY THE SPIRIT OF POVERTY, AND IT HAD BEEN PASSED DOWN FOR GENERATIONS."

After my brother told me this and several other stories, we decided to organize a family reunion at his place in Alabama, just outside of Talladega on Logan Martin Lake. We invited all of the Briggs family members, even the girls who were married and had different last names. During the reunion, we called a family meeting where I shared what the Lord had shown me about our family. Then Max and I prayed and broke the intellectual, spiritual and economic ancestral bondage off our family line.

While there were believers in our family before this time, this meeting really helped to strengthen all of their belief systems and their commitment to the Lord and the kingdom of God. Today, all of my children are believers, all of my brother Woody's children are believers, all of my brother Max's children are believers and all of my sister Sybileen's children are believers. In addition, several of our children are in ministry. My son, Tommy Jr., is in ministry; my daughter, Kerrie, and her husband are elders in their church; and my oldest daughter, Kellie, and her husband are active in their church. Several of Max's children are in ministry, and some of his grandchildren and great-grandchildren are either in ministry or headed toward ministry. I believe it was the breaking of the ancestral curse that opened the door for them to commit to the Lord and to ministry.

In addition, my siblings and I all have owned or currently own property, and all of our children have bought or are buying their own homes.

As you read this story, you might be thinking: *It could have just happened. You didn't have to break the curse.*

Yes, it *may* have happened, but it probably wouldn't have. I absolutely believe it would have never been any different in my life.

Jesus took care of all our generational iniquity when He died on the cross. He also provided for the salvation of mankind. But just as not everyone will choose salvation, not everyone will experience the relief of generational iniquity unless they apply the work of the cross to that generational iniquity. That was certainly true for us. We had to break the power of intellectual, spiritual and economic poverty off of our family line.

Ancestral bondage is real, and it was included in the work of the cross. In other words, when you find yourself behaving in a way that your parents or grandparents also behaved, in all probability you have ancestral bondage. Some people call that "generational iniquity." In my case, I discovered that economic poverty was in my family line, and I began to understand that God doesn't require us to be in poverty to do His work. Of course, economic provisions and conditions are relative to the culture we live in. But the truth remains that the Lord will provide adequately for us to accomplish the work of His kingdom.

In the early 70s, my brother, Max, and I were really at odds with one another. We had some differences of opinion that really climaxed when our mother passed away. We exchanged some harsh words about the funeral arrangements and couldn't (or wouldn't) get on the same page. We became very, very distant from one another.

> "ANCESTRAL BONDAGE IS REAL, AND IT WAS INCLUDED IN THE WORK OF THE CROSS."

Several years later, when I was pastoring at Haltom Road Baptist Church, I heard the Lord speak to me about Max. I'd made it a habit to get up early on certain days of the week, between four-thirty and five o'clock in the morning, and go down to the church to study and pray. I'd pray until about seven or seven-thirty, and then I'd have breakfast with my children and take them to school.

One morning as I was praying, I heard the Lord say: "Don't bother praying anymore until you get right with your brother."

I knew exactly what He meant. So at five-thirty in the morning, I picked up the phone and called my brother in Alabama. "Max, as I was praying this morning, the Lord said I had to get right with you," I blurted out.

"Wait," he said before I could even finish. "The Lord already told me that, and this is confirmation. You're absolutely right. It is foolish to live the way we've been living."

Before we hung up the phone, we set a date for my brother to come to Texas. A few weeks later, he drove out, and we sat in a hotel room and talked through our issues. What we discovered in that conversation was the Enemy was telling me falsehoods about what *he* was thinking, and the Enemy was telling him falsehoods about what *I* was thinking. Both of us were receiving it as truth, and it was driving us apart. The things we were upset about were very frivolous, insignificant really, but the Enemy kept them magnified for years.

> "DON'T BOTHER PRAYING ANYMORE UNTIL YOU GET RIGHT WITH YOUR BROTHER."

After we bawled and squalled and forgave each other, we talked about the things we had said to each other or thought about one another. We did this all day long until we finished. From that day in the hotel room until the day he passed away two years ago, there was nobody in this world, outside of Nancy, that I was closer to than Max.

Neither one of us ever made a major decision in our life without consulting one another or having the other one pray to see what he heard the Lord say. That included all of our moves, every pastorate he took on from that day and every pastorate or position I accepted from that day. He would get confirmation about my decisions, and I would get confirmation about his.

I believe prior to being reconciled to one another, our spiritual bondage and lack of spiritual heritage kept my brother and I from forgiving one another. Had we been exposed to the power of forgiveness through a spiritual heritage, I think we would have both done that earlier. We simply had to learn about how to forgive and break the spiritual bondage off of us.

I went to see Max in the Birmingham hospital shortly before he passed away, and we reminisced about that moment in the hotel room. We talked about how grateful we were the Lord led us to get right with one another. I just loved on him, and he loved on me. Although he was very ill, I had to come back home. He called me a week later and said, "I don't think the Lord is going to let me get well, so I want to be sure you understand you're supposed to do my funeral." Even though it was just three short months after Nancy had passed away, I went to Alabama and presided over his funeral, making sure to tell our story about getting right with one another and how important that is in life's journey.

These are just a few examples of why I'm eternally grateful to the Lord for teaching me about forgiveness. It's important to understand life is too short to live in a way that you can't face other people. If your tendency is to hold on to differences, resentment and disputes, you may find there is a generational bondage in your family line. You may not agree with their behavior, even if they're family members, but you need to love *and* forgive them.

"IT'S IMPORTANT TO UNDERSTAND LIFE IS TOO SHORT TO LIVE IN A WAY THAT YOU CAN'T FACE OTHER PEOPLE."

CHAPTER 12

I WISH I'D KNOWN TIME HAS NO REVERSE. ALL I HAVE IS TODAY.

For what is your life? It is even a vapor that appears for a little time and then vanishes away.

◦ James 4:14

While I was on staff at Restoration Church, I had a vision for part of the church building becoming a ministry center. With permission from the senior pastor, Brother Doug, I had architectural plans drawn up and started dreaming and planning for the future. My vision was that, as the church grew, we would add professional, Spirit-filled counselors to our staff and they would help pastors as well as members of the congregation find healing and restoration.

Then one day, it all changed. Brother Doug retired, and with the entrance of a new senior pastor as well as a new and different approach to ministry, the possibility of my vision becoming a reality was slim to none. I had to let the vision die. Over a period of time, I felt like my tenure at Restoration was over, and the Lord told me it was time for me to step down. So I resigned my position as an elder and associate pastor.

At the beginning of my last year at Restoration, Leah Springer, one of the Christian counselors who had been attending our church, went on staff at Gateway, a church about 10 miles north of Restoration. Shortly after she started, Leah introduced me to Bob Hamp and Linda Godsey, two of Gateway's freedom pastors. We spent the day together talking about our ministries and sharing our plans and visions for having a place for ministry and healing at our individual churches.

"ONCE AGAIN, I HAD TO PUT MY FULL TRUST IN HIM."

Shortly after I resigned from Restoration, I was invited to come on staff at Gateway. When I left the church, I had never thought about visiting Gateway, let alone coming on staff. I just knew God had led me to leave and step out in faith and wait on Him. Once again, I had to put my full trust in Him.

Pastor Bob Hamp invited me over to see Gateway's ministry center, and when I walked into the building, it was as though I was looking at *my* dream! Just as I envisioned, they had professional, Spirit-filled counselors on staff. It was just amazing!

But Nancy and I had never attended a service at Gateway, so Pastor Robert invited us to come visit one weekend to make sure we liked the church and felt comfortable. We attended a service the very next weekend. After it was over, as Nancy and I were sitting in our car in the parking lot, I looked at her and asked, "Well, what did you think?"

"It feels like home," she responded.

"You're exactly right. This is our church."

It didn't matter whether I came on staff or not; we knew this was the place God was planting us.

While I was still trying to decide whether or not to accept the offer, Pastor Robert invited me to a staff meeting where Pastor Jack Hayford was speaking. As the Lord began to move during the staff meeting, Pastor Jack went around the room and put his hands on all the staff

> "THIS IS YOUR NEW ASSIGNMENT; YOU CAN TAKE IT OR LEAVE IT."

members. Because he didn't know who I was or whether I was on staff or not, he laid his hands on me and prayed for me. As he did, I heard the Lord say: "This is your new assignment; you can take it or leave it."

I got up off of my knees and said, "I'll take it."

I met with Pastor Tom Lane and Pastor Brady Boyd and accepted the position. I hadn't planned on this happening. I was just ready for my next assignment. Proverbs 16:9 says, "A man's heart plans his way, but the Lord directs his steps." God had planted a vision and a dream in my heart and I had a plan, but it wasn't until I allowed the Lord to direct my steps — to show me the way — that the dream became a reality.

As believers, we need to live each day allowing the Lord to direct our steps. We only have today. *No one* is promised tomorrow. That does not mean we can't plan and look forward to the future, but we should embrace today and each moment. We shouldn't waste a minute of the time we have.

Having been raised in an atmosphere of poverty, I developed an attitude of always looking forward to a better day. In the first grade, I remember learning so many new and foreign concepts such as using proper English and not using the word "ain't." I began to think: *if I can just make it through the first grade, life will really be easier.* In many ways it was easier, but then it was ... *if I can just make it through elementary school ... if I can just make it through high school ... if I can just make it through the Air Force ... if I*

> "WE ONLY HAVE TODAY. NO ONE IS PROMISED TOMORROW."

can just make it through college … and so on. I was not able to live in the present, but rather, I was always looking toward the future. I'm convinced I missed many moments of revelation and understanding about life by not living every day to the fullest.

At this present season of my life, I now live in the moment, enjoying it more than the one before. I also have a deeper understanding of the exhortation the Scriptures give us for living each day to the fullest. Hebrews 3:8 says, "Today, if you hear His voice, do not harden your hearts." And Matthew 6:33–34 says, "But seek first the kingdom of God and His righteousness, and all these things shall be added to you. Therefore do not worry about tomorrow, for tomorrow will worry about its own things. Sufficient for the day is its own trouble."

I believe it is the purpose of the Lord for us to live each day, doing the best we can, with what we have in this moment. We should enjoy today, have fun and do His will and purpose.

There's a misconception that we can do tomorrow what we should do today. James 4:14 (NLT), says, "How do you know what your life will be like tomorrow? Your life is like the morning fog — it's here a little while, then it's gone." If you don't start on it today, don't count on doing it tomorrow. There's a Spanish proverb that says, "Tomorrow is often the busiest day of the week."

I wish someone had taken me aside when I was young and guided me into thinking about what I wanted to do with my life. I had a passion and a strong drive to finish school and go to college. I really considered myself someone who wanted to get ahead and get a formal education, but at the time, I didn't think about what

God's purpose was for my life. And I didn't grasp how rapidly time moved. If just one person had said to me, "Tommy, you don't realize it now, but time moves *very* quickly. You really need to think about what you want to do with your life. Tomorrow will be here before you know it," then I think the Lord would have had an opportunity to speak to me, and I would have avoided a lot of disappointment.

High school, the Air Force, college, seminary … it all moved so rapidly. I spent all those years trying to find my identity. As I look back on that time, I wish someone had sat me down and said, "You blink your eyes a couple of times and your life will be over. You really need to think seriously about your future."

I wish someone had told me it's important to dream big and make a difference in this world. You are here for a unique destiny. Find it and have fun along the way, living to the fullest. It's up to you to make the most of this life.

When I was younger, I had more of a survival mentality than anything else. Now, as I think about the time flying by and enjoying the moment, I think about my grandson, Adam, whom we lost to cancer. We had no idea he was only going to be with us for a little over three years, yet in his short stay on this earth, he made an impact on so many lives.

> "WE WOULD HAVE PACKED ADDITIONAL THINGS INTO THE DAYS WE HAD LEFT AND REALLY ENJOYED ONE ANOTHER."

You *cannot* go back. Time moves too fast. You need to enjoy every moment with your spouse, your children and your grandchildren. You need to make the most out of your relationships and value the people in your life.

Since Nancy has passed away, I've gained a better understanding that you can't go backward and you can't undo things. If I could, I would have lived life fuller with her. There are some additional fun things we would have done. While I don't have any major regrets, if I could have just comprehended the value of our time together, we would have packed additional things into the days we had left and really enjoyed one another. Once you're beyond that point, as I am today, and take a backward look, you realize how much you really missed.

One way to live your life to the fullest is to have your mind clear and open to the revelation of the Lord every day of your life. This happened to me on Sunday night, August 22, 2010 — just ten days after Nancy passed away. I had a lingering ache as I wondered, and almost doubted, about whether or not Nancy was okay.

I cried out to the Lord, "Nancy and I served you all of our married life together, but I want to know if Nancy is okay."

In the middle of the night, He gave me a revelation — a vision — that put my heart at ease and gave me peace for the rest of my days. At one o'clock in the morning, I woke up wide awake. I got up and went to the bathroom, then I returned to my bed and just laid there, fully awake and unable to go back to sleep. I was tempted to turn on the television, but instead I chose to listen to scripture on CD. As I began listening, I sensed the Lord's presence and believed He wanted to show me something.

"YOU ARE HERE FOR A UNIQUE DESTINY."

I began seeing a vision. It was as though I was standing outside of myself. (Two scriptural accounts of visions are in the New Testament in Acts 10:10 and Acts 22:17.) During everything that I saw next, I was awake and conscious of being at home in my bed without Nancy. I was not asleep.

Nancy was in the hospital room at Baylor Grapevine where she had been pronounced dead. I was sitting by her bedside (which is where I was when she passed away) with a doctor who had to remain with me for a short period of time after her death. He was sitting in a chair completing his paperwork, and there were two nurses outside her room at the nurses' station.

I saw Nancy's finger move and then her arm moved slightly. The doctor explained that sometimes after death the body's nervous system causes the body to move and twitch. Then I noticed her lips were moving, so I leaned in to get closer to her, and she said, "I love you."

"I love you too," I replied.

I turned to the doctor and said, "She just spoke to me!"

The doctor refuted me, saying, "No, she could not possibly be speaking to you."

I argued with him, insisting that she did speak to me. He turned away and left the room.

Once again, I leaned in close to Nancy's face.

"What gown do I have on?" she asked me.

I described it to her, and then she requested I get her another gown from her closet. I went to the closet and there was a very beautiful long, white gown similar to her wedding dress.

"How much do I weigh?" she asked me.

"One hundred thirty-five pounds, just like the day we were married," I responded.

After I helped her change her gown, I decided I should tell the nurses and the doctor what was happening. I went to the door of the hospital room and looked out. No one was there. I returned to Nancy's bed, and she started talking to me again.

"I'd like to sit up," she said.

"Well Honey, I don't know if you should."

"Help me, please."

So I pulled her up and she sat on the side of the bed.

Then she said, "I'd like to walk, will you help me?"

And so I lifted her up, and she stood. When she stood up, she said, "Let me go, I'm okay."

"SHE LOOKED LIKE SHE DID WHEN WE WERE FIRST MARRIED, GLOWING IN HER WHITE WEDDING DRESS."

She started walking around the room, and then she turned around toward me. She was radiant! She was smiling and full of life. She looked like she did when we were first married, glowing in her white wedding dress.

"I have no more pain!" she said as she looked at me.

"Hallelujah! We have our miracle! You have been resurrected from the dead!" I shouted with joy!

"Yes, yes," she replied, and then she began laughing.

Suddenly, I sat up in bed, believing I had Nancy by the hand only to discover I was holding onto one of her pillows. When the vision was over, I clearly heard the Lord say, "I wanted to let you know your wife is okay. And I wanted to reassure you that your faith is real."

I got out of bed (by this time it was three o'clock in the morning) and wrote down everything the Lord had revealed to me. The Bible says, "Faith is the substance of things hoped for, the very evidence of things not seen" (Hebrews 11:1). I believe I was allowed to see Nancy in her resurrected state in order to strengthen my faith. Since that time, I know God's peace has been in me.

Two days after this happened, I called all of my children on a conference call and told them about the vision I had. That was the first vision I can verifiably know was a vision because I was *totally* awake, yet at the same time I was literally in the hospital room.

I have to say I long to wake up and discover that Nancy's still here and we can enjoy each other and live life together. I'm not regretting; I'm simply trying to emphasize the importance of living every day of your life to the fullest.

As I enter into the sunset time of my life, I realize how important it is to open myself up to hear the Lord every day and to practice His presence in the midst of having fun and connecting with people. You cannot go back. You have to go forward. That's why it's vital to enjoy the people around you and not take them for granted. Take every opportunity you have to be around somebody you love, especially close friends and family. Live out every moment to the fullest. Time has no reverse. All you have is today.

"TAKE EVERY OPPORTUNITY YOU HAVE TO BE AROUND SOMEBODY YOU LOVE"

ABOUT THE AUTHOR

TOMMY H. BRIGGS, SR. serves as one of the Freedom Pastors at Gateway Church in Dallas/Fort Worth, Texas. He has been in ministry for 53 years and has been at Gateway for six years. He received his bachelor's degree from Samford University in Birmingham, Alabama, and his Master of Theology from New Orleans Baptist Theological Seminary. He has pastored churches in Louisiana, Alabama and Texas, and has ministered in the area of freedom throughout the United States and in Africa, China, Cyprus, Egypt, Guatemala, India, Honduras, Israel, Lebanon and Slovakia for more than 25 years. Tommy has three married children and 10 grandchildren. Follow him on twitter @briggssr.